Praise

MW00531922

"History, psychology, and magic blend nicely in this equine book of spells from Lawren Leo (*Dragonflame*), a spiritual counselor, and Domenic Leo, a former art history professor at Duquesne University. Drawing from a variety of traditions, . . . the authors present a vast array of spells and rituals intended to furnish a better understanding of the ways the spirit of the horse acts upon everyday human life. Each spell includes explanations of steps and supplies, as well as information about specific horse archetypes and spirits involved in the ritual. For instance, the jade horse of Chinese mythology promotes good luck . . . while the winged horse of Greek mythology can be a catalyst for lucid dreaming. Though 'no contact with actual horses is required' for these rituals, this enchanting guide provides pleasant reflective rituals for contemplating the connection between horses and humans."

**—*Publishers Weekly***

"Carefully researched and delightfully written, Leo's book brings to life the core energy of ancient horse magick. Enjoy the ride as you welcome, empower, and guide your inner shaman. Myth, magick, spells, chants, rituals, and practical information gallop across the page to promote, challenge, and enhance your true essence. Powerful and profound, a tool to help choose and shape your destiny, you will love this marvelous book!"

**—Silver RavenWolf, author of**
***To Ride a Silver Broomstick* and many
other books of magick**

"Imagine the strength and beauty of the amazing horse, and then imagine that power combined with magick. This is the gift that *Horse Magick* brings to the reader. You don't have to love horses to appreciate their spirit and mythological importance, but I suspect that you will after reading this book. A long overdue addition to the genre."

**—Deborah Blake, author of**
*The Little Book of Cat Magic*

"Horses clearly possess potent magic. If you've ever tuned into their wise stillness, gentle strength, and unbridled freedom, you're going to love *Horse Magick*. Read it to expand your magical repertoire and deepen your understanding of the symbolic and historical importance of horses, while liberating your spirit and stepping into your power in the process."

**—Tess Whitehurst, author of**
*Unicorn Magic*

"The brothers Leo have crafted the definitive guide to equine magick and myth. Drawing from magickal traditions around the world, *Horse Magick* offers a stunning survey of the role that horses have played throughout history. Lawren and Domenic artfully retell stories hailing from Japan to ancient Greece, and from the Americas to Africa. Each chapter is enriched by the addition of practical, simple, and effective spells—each and every one explained in detail so the practitioner can understand not only the *how* but also the *why* of magickal practice. This book is for more than just horse lovers; it is a delight to read and will inspire magicians for generations to come."

**—Nicholas Pearson, author of**
*Crystal Basics* **and** *Stones of the Goddess*

"*Horse Magick* has taken me on an enthralling mystical, magical, and historical journey from ancient to modern times alongside the astonishing, majestic horse. Extensively researched and eloquently presented, Lawren Leo and Domenic Leo summon their readers around the world, in order to grasp and appreciate the concepts of how mythology meets and melds with historical realities. We learn that, throughout time, the immeasurable contributions of horses, and other equine species, have always played a significant role both magically and as a workforce, while aiding deities and helping the advancement of humankind. As an added bonus, this book is abundant with magical spells and incantations for an array of various situations, and they will certainly be incorporated into my own practice. Personally, I am now enchanted by the spirit of the horse. A captivating, educational read, and truly created as a labor of love!"

—**Miss Aida, author of**
***Hoodoo Cleansing and Protection Magic***

"In *Horse Magick*, the Leo brothers teach us new perspectives through spells, rituals, chants, and meditations. The way they cover symbolism and archetypes is simply delicious—there is no other word to describe it. The book's rituals are practical and easy to perform. For all those who dedicate yourselves to the most ceremonial and ritual forms of magic, this book is a refreshing balm to help you recall that magic is much simpler and that simplicity and wit are your two weapons of power. If you have not previously held a book of magic and sorcery in your hands, *Horse Magick* is a good place to start, as it is modern, practical, and clear. For those with more experience in this field, *Horse Magick* will make you rethink everything you think you know. *Horse Magick* is essential for every modern wizard or sorcerer."

—**Elhoim Leafar, author of**
***The Magical Art of Crafting Charm Bags***

"*Horse Magick* is an entrancing journey from prehistoric horse ancestors to ancient Greek wars; a journey to our highest potential through the spirit of the horse, the embodiment of freedom. The visuals alone take you on an enchanting trip through time, and the book's extensive collection of spells is captivating, whether you grew up riding or have only seen photos of horses. Grab this book for an alluring view from horseback. Through the tides, deep in the rain forest, or through war-torn landscapes, let the horse be your guide."

**—Amy Blackthorn, author of**
***Blackthorn's Botanical Magic* and *Sacred Smoke***

"*Horse Magick* is sure to bring strength, vitality, and empowerment into all aspects of your life. Through tapping into the symbolism and spirit of equine energy, the Leo brothers show you how to harness this force into your magickal practice to yield fantastic results. This approachable, clever, and well-researched book will assist you in getting your magick to work at full horsepower!"

**—Mat Auryn, author of**
***Psychic Witch: A Metaphysical Guide***
***to Meditation, Magick, and Manifestation***

# HORSE
# MAGICK

*Spells and Rituals for
Self-Empowerment,
Protection, and
Prosperity*

LAWREN LEO with DOMENIC LEO, PhD

WEISER BOOKS

# DEDICATION

*For our beloved parents, who gave us our first horses.*

---

This edition first published in 2020 by Weiser Books, an imprint of
Red Wheel/Weiser, LLC
With offices at:
65 Parker Street, Suite 7
Newburyport, MA 01950
*www.redwheelweiser.com*

ISBN: 978-1-57863-698-3
Library of Congress Cataloging-in-Publication Data
available upon request.

Cover design by Kasandra Cook
Cover image by Shutterstock
Interior photos/images by Nathaniel Dailey
Interior by Steve Amarillo / Urban Design LLC
Typeset in Adobe Bembo and Trajan

Printed in the United States of America
IBI
10  9   8  7   6   5   4   3   2   1

# CONTENTS

# ACKNOWLEDGMENTS

The idea for this book was born during a conversation with Judika Illes about our mutual love of horses and magick, at which time invisible hooves first struck ground. Shortly thereafter, research, meditation, and writing commenced in earnest. But equestrian Beverly Tarbell Patrick is responsible for introducing my brother and me to horses, riding, and Pony Club, and for giving years of mentoring and friendship in and out of the ring. We are grateful to both for their help, advice, and support.

Researching a book as wide-ranging as *Horse Magick* necessitated input from writers and scholars and professionals in wildly diverse fields, covering history, literature, anthropology, mythology, philology, zoology, crystals, genetics, fashion, and psychology. We would also like to mention and thank those who were kind enough to offer important, thought-provoking leads: Marie DeFeo, Judy Hall, Kerry Handron, Marlene Hennessy, Stacey Pierson, Sarah Thal, and Olga Zakharova-Kaetano. And, without a doubt, the spirit of Voodoo Queen Marie Laveau was one of the main occult driving forces behind this book.

# ABOUT THIS BOOK

Thriving or extinct, real or mythical, familiar or little-known, each manifestation of Horse Spirit offers magickal powers. I have designed *Horse Magick* to embrace the 21st-century spirit of globalism and have tried to direct its spells to the most pressing issues of our times—from self-esteem, anxiety, and substance abuse to gender issues and social media. Specifically, I have written this book in a nonlinear fashion to allow readers to delve into any chapter or any spell that corresponds to their individual needs, be they love, money, or empowerment in a world filled with social injustice and misunderstanding. You can go directly to the most appropriate spell and use it following the simple instructions. Nothing further is required!

If, however, you prefer a more in-depth approach, *Horse Magick* joins magick with studies in art history, archaeology, literature, and folklore at the beginning of each chapter. It identifies and describes potent examples from worldwide and historical cultures to expand your vocabulary of spellwork. In this way, I show how you can use specific deities to control the "inner horse" we all have—a trustworthy spiritual ally.

To broaden your knowledge, my brother brings to light a host of horse deities, both time-honored and forgotten, and discusses them for the first time in clear language, despite the esoteric context. He documents his research carefully, giving you ample opportunity to pursue the topics in ancient myths and literature, in the writings of ancient and modern historians, and through examples of related art, architecture, and sculpture.

My brother and I have jointly written on the art of practicing magick with Horse Spirit from two different perspectives. Our combined points of view can help improve your magickal success rate by offering access to a rich body of knowledge based on primary-source research—research based on original documents, myths, and prayers, rather than secondhand resources, which are often based in opinion.

In this book, I guide you through original spells, chants, and meditations that are based on knowledge I gained as an initiate in clandestine mystery schools. My contributions include instructions on how to use magick for love, prosperity, astral travel, protection, and curse-breaking. My spells defy stylistic description and draw on multiple sources from high magick and Wicca, classics in literature and folklore, and, most important, my personal psychic experiences.

I also offer spells for bonding with and protecting your animals, as well as for remembering those who have passed to the other side. The spells in this book are designed to make you look within; your inner world is the source of all magick! When used properly, the spells awaken the latent symbolism of Horse Spirit. This energy existed as a primal force *before* humanity appeared on planet Earth. The power of Horse Spirit is akin to that of Jungian archetypes. Indeed, we encounter the importance of the horse—and sometimes even distinct and surprising similarities— in myths from all times and places.

In chapter 22, I give a variety of spells that can be performed quickly and still promote, challenge, and enhance deeper thinking. If you are busy and need a powerful, yet convenient, solution to a dilemma, these quick and profound spells may give you just what you require. They are inspired by and based on idioms, proverbs, and phrases centered around horses and are designed to be performed more quickly than usual. With each, I offer additional information describing why I chose certain magickal ingredients and correspondences so that you have not only a fast yet effective spell, but also a ready-made reference guide and a chance to return to the spell after you have performed it so you can delve more deeply into its meaning.

I end the book with a dictionary that will help you interpret your equine dreams. This dictionary combines traditions including my cultural heritage of *stregheria* (Italian witchcraft), the psychoanalytic schools of C. G. Jung and Sigmund Freud, superstition, folklore, and personal experience.

## Literary Background

As Judika Illes, author of *Encyclopedia of 5,000 Spells,* brought to my attention in a discussion some years ago, there is no formal history or compilation of horse-related magick. British author Mary Gertrude Oldfield Howey wrote the only book devoted to horses and magick in 1923, *The Horse in Magic and Myth.* She was following a venerable tradition of creating grand, historical overviews, with compilations of anecdotes taken from worldwide history, myth, and folklore. The title can, however, be misleading; hers is not a spellbook.

Generations later, in 1993, Ted Andrews published *Animal Speak.* By this time, a new genre had evolved that included Wicca and the practice of earth-based religions. His revolutionary series of books concentrated on teaching readers about bonding with animal totems. Moving in a new direction, D. J. Conway departed from the Native American tradition and explored Western European mythology. Conway's new perspective, exemplified in her 1995 book, *Animal Magick,* was carried forward in her 2018 compilation, *Magickal Mystical Creatures: Invite Their Powers into Your Life.*

Yet, perhaps ironically, it is Tarl Warwick's 2017 revised edition of Robert Means Lawrence's 1898 *The Magic of the Horse Shoe with Other Folklore Notes* that remains the most succinct treatment of the subject. Numerous other publications have touched on isolated elements of horse magick, but none concentrate solely on it. *Horse Magick* returns to Oldfield's focus on horse magick, but moves beyond both the Native American and Western European traditions.

This book is not intended as an exhaustive history of the horse. If this subject interests you, I highly recommend the comprehensive and readable 2015 publication by Wendy Williams, *The Horse: The Epic History of Our Noble Companion,* as well as J. Edward Chamberlin's 2006 *How the Horse Has Shaped Civilizations* and Gerald and Loretta Hausman's 2003 book, *The Mythology of Horses: Horse Legend and Lore throughout the Ages*, which, although it alludes to magick, remains distinctly secular. You will find other recommended readings targeted on the topics discussed at the end of each chapter.

# INTRODUCTION

*The primordial image, or archetype, is a figure—*
*be it a daemon, a human being, or a process.*

Carl Jung

As a practicing magician and witch, there is a rule that I have found to be true within the world of spells and magick: When a sincere desire and a force from Mother Nature combine to inspire your magick, it becomes more powerful. After all, everything mystical and occult (hidden) is already gestating within our subconscious, just waiting for us to bring it to life, to reawaken it. But there must be something that sets this into action. For some, it may be using a seal or sigil. For others, it may be as simple as meditating by the ocean or a body of water that emits negative ions, like a waterfall. For myself, I have learned to evoke the strongest powers through inspiration, which I find most often in my interactions with animals—in this case, the horse and its herd. The human-animal bond can be symbiotic, imparting mutual benefits on the physical, emotional, mental, spiritual, and psychic levels. Do not underestimate it.

A single horse, even at an early age, is powerful enough to trample, cripple, and even kill. Now, imagine the power behind a herd of fully grown horses. The adrenaline rush that drives the pounding hooves of a herd in motion exists on a plane that is accessible to us—the plane that psychologist C. G. Jung called the "collective unconscious." This plane is also known as the astral realm, which holds all equine energy and where archetypes come alive. In *Horse Magick*, you will work with extremely powerful spells, rituals, chants, and meditations that ignite your subconscious mind and connect it with the energy of the horse and herd.

It is a commonly held belief throughout the world that each animal, rock, stone, and piece of nature has a spirit or spirits that preside over it. It is also part of a universal creed that the gods and goddesses, faery folk, and myriad mythological beasts live within us, somewhere deep in the folds of our subconscious minds and our personal astral realms. *Horse Magick* points the way to these spirits or daemons, which range from earthy and coarse figures like dragons and the Russian witch Baba Yaga, to more delicate and refined archetypes like the ancient Greek Muses and the winged horse Pegasus. The horse's totemic, energetic power is tied to saints, mythological beasts, elementals and faery folk, Voodoo, and ancient gods and goddesses, some of whom have remained obscure until now and were, for the most part, rarely used in ritual work. Whichever totem, energy, or archetype you choose, *Horse Magick* offers the guidance and knowledge you need to challenge your deeper thinking and help you meet your magickal goals.

Our world is filled with social injustice—to the point where it has become difficult for the true self to emerge. But the 21st century is ripe with change, and magick is now a necessary and fitting remedy for the disempowered. This is especially true in our present era, as we witness the move away from restrictive definitions of gender and struggle to annihilate lifestyle labels. For activists ready to become arbiters of justice, or for seekers ready to learn new spells, *Horse Magick* can provide a problem-solving grimoire that draws on the ultimate symbol of freedom, passion, and power—the horse.

This book seeks to revivify that power. Don't discard that special dream that never reached fruition or that certain someone or something you have sought! You can bring this all back in a healthy, balanced way as something new. Energy is inherently indestructible; you can only banish or change it. *Horse Magick* teaches you how to manifest new desires, dreams, and goals by using crystals, herbs, essential oils, and the Tarot. Actual contact with horses is not required. With these magickal items and in conjunction with spells, rites, and meditations, you can harness horse power in its most refined and controllable forms.

The book contains a storehouse of original spells that resonate with the distinctive energies of the 21st-century collective consciousness. I have carefully crafted them to retain the ancient and undefinable mystique and allure of various occult forces from the earliest origins of witchcraft, drawing on traditional as well as progressive currents of magick that allow me to teach them in a truly intimate and manageable fashion. No chapter depends on the others. Feel free to dip into one chapter to discover little-known deities like the Egypto-Canaanite Reshef. Then try another to learn new information about popular mythological creatures like centaurs and Pegasus. I have tried to keep the text user-friendly, with clear and concise directions for the spells and ample explanation of the symbolism and significance of all elements in them, from numerology to essential oils.

As you work with Horse Spirit, you may begin dreaming of all things equine in nature. This is the power of the horse totem flowing through your subconscious mind to help further develop and refine your psychic, magickal, and spiritual gifts. To help you learn from these dreams, I end the book with a dictionary of terms for interpreting equine dreams. Use it to help understand your dreams. Let it guide you as you fill your grimoire and journal with illuminations and begin to understand the nature of your power as an energy worker, witch, and magician. Dreams are the doorways to our inner world and memory palace.

*Horse Magick* utilizes the energy behind the symbol of the horse as it appears in the guise of the many deities it inspired around the world and throughout the ages. In fact, while researching this book, I found that each new horse breed, deity, and work of art opened a floodgate of stimulation. This manifested in the form of new magick (horse magick). Learn how to call on the energy of these deities and associated forces individually and collectively. The horse, a creature that lives in a herd, reminds us that we are not alone and that we should not alienate others. The great, fierce mare proves that we are always loved. The powerful stallion offers us a timeless source of leadership. Their procreative urges and raw sexuality teach us to love and respect our bodies and the gifts of sex and sexuality. By becoming one with equine energy, we find empowerment in all aspects of our lives, as well as the promise that positive change is not just for you, the practitioner, but for our posterity and our great planet, Mother Earth.

*Chapter 1*

---

# HORSE SPIRIT AND HORSE MAGICK

The essence of Horse Spirit is freedom. It is a noble and resilient force, with limitless energy at its core. The horse's intimate relation with Spirit and nature, clear in all global polytheistic religions, and the easy access it provides as intermediary to both are compelling reasons to use equine magick.

The moment you mount a horse, this animal becomes a physical intermediary between the world beneath you and the unknown dimensions above. Horse Spirit can accompany you on an adrenaline-charged, exhilarating journey. "Once a horse is let loose," Xenophon tells us in *On Horsemanship* (X § 9–15), "its movement tends by nature towards swiftness, in which it takes great pleasure." Hooves pound and clods of earth fly in all directions as the horse suspends you between earth and sky. The force propels you on a race through time into the future. The air resists you, but your hair streaks in unison with the horse's whipping mane. Your past remains behind in hoofprints and clouds of dust. You become acutely aware of savoring the moment; you embrace the present; you create your future.

As you ride, the horse's moments of contact with the earth jolt through your bones. The rhythm releases you from gravity as you sense the pulse of life and death—at once earth's gift and her mystery—and then enter a trancelike state that takes you out of time. The sonic insistence fragments your primal urges, and you experience an unfamiliar state of freedom; you come to know what you need. As you unite with Horse Spirit, you become strong, filled with power. You surmount your fear of the future and no longer doubt your ability to shape it, to manipulate your own destiny. No bridle or saddle is necessary. Your equine guide calls for nothing beyond your own will.

To conjure, contain, and manipulate the energy we call "horse" presents challenges. But when we study its avatars, we are rewarded with the discovery and awareness of ourselves—our psychic talents and limitations, our desire for purity of purpose and clarity of goal. Horse Spirit freely offers us a way to better our temporal lives by transforming our human spirits. It grants us the use of its physical attributes and personality traits as portals to dimensions where change is a reality, not a concept. The manifestation of this force on earth—its action within the physical dimension we perceive in time—provides much-needed supplements that can help us to live well-balanced lives.

There was a time when we were all free of burdens, when we did not even know the definition of the word "burden." But something peculiar happens to us after childhood. We fall prey to the pressures of society, and then may feel the need to take on extra responsibilities. We often do this without reflecting on what will happen as a consequence. Extra responsibilities can create burdens that hold us in emotional bondage. These emotions do not serve a purpose. They enslave us and prevent us from experiencing healthy, fulfilling lives. These everyday burdens, however, are an outcome of our conscious and subconscious decisions. That means that they consist of energy and can be changed. If you find yourself playing a role rather than living a life, this Freedom Spell can play a critical function in your well-being.

# SPELL FOR FREEDOM FROM BURDENS AND STRESS

In this spell, you ask Horse Spirit to set your own spirit free. This can alter the state of your spirit, which then returns revivified, permitting you to find the strength you need to eliminate a burden. This spell has the ability to restore your resilience, make you healthier, and redirect your motivation. It is also useful for those suffering from anxiety, substance abuse of any type, and the disease of addiction.

***What you need:***
All you need for this spell is a comfortable chair to sit on or bed to lie on.

***Instructions:***
Commit the spell to memory. Chant it rhythmically. The trick is to lull yourself gently into what's called an alpha state—a state in which you are half asleep and half awake, as when you just wake up in the morning and still feel drowsy. To help achieve this state, imagine a white candle burning with a peaceful, unwavering flame in your mind's eye. Hold your concentration on that image while you chant:

> *Mane tossed through rushing air,*
> *No one around to glance or stare.*
>
> *Jumping proudly hoof to ground,*
> *Awaken the spirit inside me bound.*
>
> *Gallop fast, take hold of me;*
> *Let me remember when I was free.*

Don't get hung up on how many times you chant it. Just chant. You can do this lying down in bed or sitting in a comfortable armchair. Chant it as many times as you like, whether for one day or three weeks, whatever feels right to you. Allow the spirit of the horse to lead you to a sanctuary, to a place where your emotional bondage will be removed.

When you first read the spell, envision the imagery of a galloping horse in your mind's eye. Then, slowly transition to a point where you chant the spell and only see the lit white candle and "feel" the intent of the words.

**Tip:**

The trick is to place the "idea" of freedom into your subconscious mind via the alpha state. In other words, chant until you almost fall asleep, while trying to sense the overall intention of the spell—freedom. When you're finished, say this affirmation:

*Now, all burdens have been removed safely and securely.*

**Additional resources**

Xenophon, *The Works of Xenophon*, trans. H. G. Dakyns, vol. 3, part 2, Three Essays: On the Duties of a Cavalry General, On Horsemanship, and On Hunting (London: Macmillan and Co., 1897). Retrieved from https://archive.org (accessed 9/26/2019).

*Chapter 2*

# THE HORSE IN PREHISTORY

Horse Spirit embodies the concept of evolutionary progression for the sake of adaptation. The horse manifested on earth and changed dramatically over unimaginable stretches of time. We know this because paleontologists have been able to document transformations in the horse's bodily structure with extreme precision through a wealth of fossil remains. Moreover, there is a unique energetic power source that derives from the streamlined process of this creature's evolution. Unlike the subtle energies associated with change in the plant world, Horse Spirit is raw and formidable. It is dynamic. Its limbs, neck, teeth, and hooves morphed in quantum leaps and bounds. In the prehistoric era, fifty million years ago, the incarnation of Horse Spirit was soft and vulnerable, agile and spry. Experts have named this tender creature *eohippus*, which means "the dawn horse."

*Skeletal foot of eohippus in a prehistoric rainforest.*

## Eohippus, the Dawn Horse

Eohippus was the size of a fifty-pound dog. Forty-five to fifty million years ago, it lived in great numbers in vast stretches of canopied rainforest in what is now North America, foraging on leaves rather than grass. Archaeologists have found many fossils in the Wind River Basin in Wyoming. Apart from its size, the characteristic that distinguishes eohippus most from the modern horse is its foot, which had four soft, pad-like toes with proto-hooves on its forelegs and three toes on its longer hind legs. This feature gave eohippus sensitivity to the moist, loose ground cover. But over millions of years, changes in the earth's climate reduced the size of the rainforest habitat, exposing the forest dwellers to new terrain—grasslands, sandy prairies, and rocky steppes. This new terrain made speed necessary for survival, for it was popu-lated by numerous fierce predators. As a result, the central toes of eohippus hardened, while the side toes shrank until they became mere trace bones. And this was just the beginning of a long chain of evolutionary metamorphoses.

# The People of the Caves

The earliest human records we have of horses predate the invention of writing by millennia. In fact, the images are so far removed from us in time that they are stripped of nearly all original context, and their purpose remains a mystery.[1] They date to a period near the end of the Ice Age, around 25,000 BCE, when present-day Europe was partially buried under vast glaciers.

Prehistoric peoples, including the Cro-Magnons, led nomadic lives as hunter-gatherers and sometimes took shelter in extensive cave complexes. They painted a striking group of lifesize, leopard-spotted horses on the walls of a cave in Pech Merle in Cabrerets, present-day southern France. These cave paintings are not "art" as we may understand it—that is, as something that serves an aesthetic, decorative function in a home or institution. Rather, they are akin to "sacred art" we might encounter in a place of worship—that is, as something meant to lift the mind from the physical to the spiritual realm. Cave paintings in general are not usually found in living quarters, but rather in hard-to-reach locales, energetically charged areas where neither light nor sound could penetrate. For example, in another French site, Lascaux, paintings are completely hidden in a well shaft located deep in a cave and accessible only with great difficulty.

One plausible interpretation for the horse paintings at Pech Merle is that they were meant to serve as a magickal aid to hunting. This theory is supported by the fact that there are nicks in the surface of the cave wall, suggesting that spears were hurled at the images of the horses. Indeed, there may have been a shaman or painter who acted as an intermediary between the real and spirit worlds—a role that, despite a common misperception, may have been filled by either a man or a woman. A striking element of the Pech Merle paintings is the incorporation of handprints all around, and in some places superimposed upon, the horses. These outlines were created by spitting a fine spray of mud over the hand. The act itself was ritualistic, leaving breath and saliva on the wall, joining the person creating the mark with the image and the land. A group of experts has advanced the theory that the size of the handprints indicates that women made these marks.[2]

No matter the gender of their creators, these paintings designate the places as magickally charged areas—power zones, places where human and animal spirits could meet. In one site, the painters returned to the difficult-to-access location generation after generation to paint images one atop the other. This leads some to believe that the images were not revered. I believe that, to the contrary, it indicates that making and interacting with the paintings were the paramount actions. Each successive creation of the images, whether of animals or of hands, integrated the participants individually and the clan collectively into a cultural, shared memory. These early artists were contacting Horse Spirit in the deep, secret recesses of the earth to assist in their survival. The light they brought in small oil lamps was as symbolic as it was necessary.

I feel strongly that a small group of people used these caves as a safe haven, a place in which to create a spiritual vortex, to call on and gain the favor of Horse Spirit. There, they built up the courage to hunt the speedy horse for food, and to acquire the necessary mental stamina to confront the dangerous stallion who led the herd. They were aware that the cave provided psychological, spiritual, emotional, and mental preparation for the world outside.

The quest for leadership and the passing on of generational knowledge in the presence of Horse Spirit was the driving force behind assembling in this place. The clan needed to learn how to react properly in dangerous situations, how to control volatile forces, to adapt quickly to ensure survival, and to work as a team. Above all, they were in the cave to receive information from a spiritual force, to help with a life-or-death situation. In short, they were there to learn survival tactics. The outcome of the ceremony was bravery tempered by respect for the primal force of nature, and this is the key to the two spells that follow.

# INITIATION OF HORSE SPIRIT

This first spell is especially effective to consecrate a new space or reconsecrate an existing space. This includes the sacred space within you, the area where your magick is nurtured and where it can safely develop under the protection of Horse Spirit.

*What you need:*
The Hermit card and the Death card from a tarot deck—Major Arcana IX and XIII, respectively. You will also need sage incense (cone or stick) or sage (any variety).

*Instructions:*
To begin, remove all items from your altar or sacred space. Clean it thoroughly. Place the Hermit card in the center. Light the sage/ sage incense and place it in front of the Hermit card. Now, take the Death card (face up) and begin to fan the incense smoke slowly—three strokes toward you, then three strokes away from you. Repeat the three-and-three stroke action while chanting:

> *Bring me to the sacred cave;*
>
> *Nurturing growth is what I crave.*
>
> *Spirits to this space attached*
>
> *Give me power as I'm hatched;*
>
> *Bravery, wisdom, leadership, force,*
>
> *I thank you Spirit of the Horse.*

When finished, place the Death card on the altar underneath the Hermit card. Let them sit for twenty-four hours.

Why did I choose the Hermit card? In a traditional tarot deck, the Hermit represents introspection, self-reflection, and a sacred place—a vortex where illumination and psychic energies lie hidden, waiting to be awakened.

Why did I choose the Death card? In a traditional tarot deck, Death represents endings and beginnings. In this case, you are harnessing its power to "bring death" to all that is stale, stagnant, and no longer necessary. Also, in most tarot decks, this card bears a picture of a black horse. Once again, a herald of endings.

Why did I choose sage/sage incense? Sage, and the fragrance of sage, are traditionally used by Native Americans and in Europe to cleanse a space or item of unwanted or negative energies, as well as to banish evil and malevolent forces. It is also used to prepare a space for magickal rituals and blessings.

## BLESSING OF HORSE SPIRIT

The power to subdue the stallion was not the only purpose of the cave gatherings. The members of the clan also sought to imbue themselves with stallion energy and absorb the horse's defense tactics. Primal stallion energy could instill fear and catch the enemy off guard. I believe that women were thought to have the ability to quell the wild Horse Spirit and that, in a shamanic role, they could talk to Horse Spirit in the cave before the hunt. In this spell, I have chosen to adapt the words of the 23rd Psalm, because it provides the means for anyone, regardless of gender, to tap into the stallion's instincts for leadership, guidance, protection, and profound empowerment.

### What you need:
One white candle, scented or unscented (votive, pillar, or taper), virgin olive oil, and table salt.

**Instructions:**

Remove all items from your altar or sacred space and clean it thoroughly. Then place the white candle in the very center and light it with reverence. Mix a half teaspoon of virgin olive oil with two pinches of table salt in a small bowl or dish. Place the dish in front of your lit candle. Dab your right thumb into the mixture and slowly trace an equal-armed cross on the center of your forehead just above the bridge of your nose while saying:

> *I banish all evil, evil eyes, curses, negativity, upset conditions,*
> *black magick, psychic attacks, and opposition through the*
> *virtues of the equal-armed cross, and unlock my passion for*
> *leadership, guidance, and protection through the power of*
> *Horse Spirit.*

Now, with your passion unleashed, recite the following spell. You need say it only one time.

> *Stallion of the ancients, your spirit is all I need.*
>
> *Lead me to green pastures and keep me from harm;*
>
> *Instill fear in my enemies with sharp hooves and bared teeth.*
>
> *No foe escapes your wrath, neither by light of day nor*
> *dark of night;*
>
> *Your unfailing vigilance protects me from surprise attack;*
>
> *Because of you, I suffer neither hunger nor thirst,*
>
> *For you know places where I receive more sustenance*
> *than I need.*
>
> *Bless me with your primal power, forever.*

When you are finished, you may sit in silence enjoying the newfound feeling of empowerment or you may simply thank Horse Spirit and let the candle burn itself out naturally. When the wax has completely cooled, dispose of it.

Why did I choose a white candle? White is the traditional color used in magick to represent purity of intent, cleansing, spirituality, and the opposite of fear, which is courage. It is also considered neutral and therefore easily imbued with any intent if charged properly.[3]

Why did I choose virgin olive oil? Olive oil is associated with peace, wisdom, and purity of heart.

Why did I choose table salt? Salt is associated with the element of earth. It is used to cleanse and wash away evil, the evil eye, and black magick, and to ground magickal energies and intent.

## ADDITIONAL RESOURCES

The description of the evolution of the horse from eohippus is highly abbreviated and simplified here. For a recent study that elaborates on its complexity, see David J. Froehlich, "Quo vadis eohippus? The Systematics and Taxonomy of the Early Eocene Equids (Perissodactyla)," *Zoological Journal of the Linnean Society* 134 (2) (February 2002), pp. 141–256.

For an informative website with high-quality images of the cave paintings at Pech Merle, see: *http://pechmerle.com.*

### Secondary sources

Bahn, Paul, and Michel Lorblanchet. *The First Artists: In Search of the World's Oldest Art* (London: Thames and Hudson, 2017).

MacFadden, Bruce J. *Fossil Horses: Systematics, Paleobiology, and Evolution of the Family Equidae* (Cambridge, England: Cambridge University Press, 1994).

Snow, Dean. "Sexual Dimorphism in European Upper Paleolithic Cave Art," *American Antiquity* 78 (4), (2013), pp. 746–761.

## NOTES

1  The first extant depiction of a person riding a horse is on the seal of the Ur III king Šu-Sin, which dates to the late 20th century BCE. See Owen, 1991.

2  Snow, 2013.

3  To learn more about charging or blessing a candle see Leo, 2014, pp. 126–127.

*Chapter 3*

# THE ANCIENT HORSE

The horse played a prominent role in the great empires of the ancient world—Mesopotamia, Egypt, and Rome—and there are numerous horse deities in these cultures associated with warfare as well as daily life. The loose-knit group of city-states in the region of Mesopotamia, in the ancient Near East, provides a time and place to begin recording a horse-human relationship. This civilization stretched from roughly 5000 to 1750 BCE. For maximum protection and ease of commerce, the Mesopotamians built the first cities in a fertile, crescent-shaped region between the Tigris and Euphrates rivers in present-day Iraq. It was here that horses were first systematically domesticated and bred, although there is also strong evidence that the Botai culture of Kazakhstan had domesticated horses as early as 3500 BCE and that the Yamnaya, or pit-grave culture, of the Caucasus spread the use of the horse (and a Proto-Indo-European language) throughout parts of Europe, India, and Asia.[1]

The historical record begins at this point, for the Mesopotamians invented writing around 3200 BCE, and their prayers, myths, and even business transactions are preserved on baked clay tablets in cuneiform text. In fact, the oldest surviving horse-training manual comes from the Hittites, famed horsemen and charioteers. This fascinating document, which dates from 1345 BCE, is attributed to Kikkuli, "master horse trainer" of the land of Mitanni, in present-day Turkey.[2]

# Astarte and Ishtar

The peoples of Mesopotamia harnessed horses and used them primarily to drive their war chariots. In fact, no secure evidence supports the use of mounted warriors in a cavalry until after 1000 BCE. It appears, however, that these people did not initially engage in actual combat with their chariots; instead, they used them as convenient transportation on the battlefield.

The Mesopotamian religious pantheon was broad and encompassed some of the deities of Canaan, which was made up of modern-day Israel, Palestine, Jordan, Lebanon, and Syria. In fact, they associated the Canaanite goddess Astarte with their most important goddess, Ishtar. Astarte, known as the Mistress of Mares, was the goddess of war, sexual love, mothers, horses, and chariots. There are hundreds of small clay statues of her depicted as a nude woman holding her breasts. These were kept in the household to bestow fertility and good luck on those who revered them. Statues and relief sculptures of Astarte also show her in a chariot.

In a passage from the *Epic of Gilgamesh*, the hero responds to the Babylonian precursor goddess, Ishtar, when she seeks to seduce him. She tempts him with the more-than-generous offer of a lapis and gold chariot and race-winning horses.[3] When Gilgamesh rebuffs her, he insults her by recounting a list of lovers she had already taken and the way they had suffered when she left them. He compares their plight to the mistreatment of a victorious war stallion that is ordered to be whipped and restrained and then to be run and given water while overheated, making it ill.[4]

The portrayal of Ishtar in the passage discussed above is by any standards conflicted and, ultimately, misogynistic. Ishtar is both whore and mother, shamefully vengeful and parentally protective. Most likely, this tale had a "spellbinding" effect on the audience when it was read aloud or sung, promulgating the idea in this culture that a woman's sexuality needed to be feared, controlled, and manipulated. Gilgamesh literally demonizes Ishtar and treats her as an evil, insatiable seductress. The champion war horses with which she baits him are a metaphor for lust. It is only by deny-ing her advances and remaining sexually abstinent that the hero obtains power over her. By reversing Ishtar's intrigue, Gilgamesh avoids the savage emotional pain the goddess has systematically inflicted on her trail of disposable lovers.

In the spell below, I have turned this characterization of Ishtar/ Astarte on its head. I reworked the storyline and extracted the boldness and beneficial power of these goddesses to make them relevant for 21st-century witches.

# SPELL FOR SEDUCTION
# AND SELF-EMPOWERMENT

This empowerment spell is meant especially for female readers, but can be used regardless of gender or sexual orientation. At its core are rights we should all possess: the right to choose any lover and always to be treated with respect by that person.

*What you need:*
The Chariot card from a tarot deck (you can download and print one if you don't own a deck), a red candle, and lapis lazuli.

*Instructions:*
Place the red candle on your altar and light it. Then say:

> *Astarte, Mistress of the Mares, I invoke you.*
>
> *Ishtar, Queen of thunderous power, empower me,*
>
> *For you are me and I am you.*
>
> *Let me seduce whomever I wish;*
>
> *Teach me to accept pleasure;*
>
> *Teach me to satisfy my needs,*
>
> *And that my purpose is not only to satisfy the needs of others.*

Place your chosen piece of lapis lazuli next to the lit candle as an offering to Astarte and Ishtar. Then say:

*Astarte, Goddess of the Morning Star, I call on you.*

*Ishtar, Queen of thunderous power, empower me,*

*For you are me and I am you.*

*Fill my aura with your confidence;*

*Let me gain the respect of others;*

*Put all those I desire at my feet;*

*Trample those who wish to enslave me in mind, body, or spirit.*

Place the Chariot card on your altar to finish creating a symbolic "triumvirate." Then say:

*Astarte, Mistress of the Cavalry and Charioteers,*
*I invoke you.*

*Ishtar, Queen of thunderous power, empower me,*

*For you are me and I am you.*

*Allow my true self to emerge,*

*For my heart is like yours.*

*It is filled with lapis and gold.*

*I have everything to give.*

Why did I choose a red candle, lapis lazuli, and the Chariot card? Placing the red candle on your altar and lighting it are signals to the goddesses and spirits that you are ready to begin your spell. This also sends and attracts vibrations associated with the color red: aggression, lust, desire, and pleasure.

Lapis lazuli is associated with psychic empowerment, especially clairvoyance and receptivity. Also, it was crushed into a powder, mixed into a paste, and used as eye makeup to cut the glare of the sun and to enhance natural beauty in ancient Mesopotamia and Egypt, adding to the seductive power of this spell.

The Chariot card connotes movement, strength, and battle. Placing it on your altar naturally calls on the spirits of empowerment, enhancing the spell's final verses and helping you to achieve your goals.

Together, the red candle, lapis lazuli, and the Chariot card create a triple symbol of magickal authority.

# Reshef

Egyptians were in contact with Mesopotamia through trade and war. This is how Astarte and another foreign horse deity, Reshef, entered their pantheon in the New Kingdom under the pharaoh Amenhotep II (1427–1401 BCE or 1427–1397 BCE). There is text on an engraved stone plinth near the Great Sphinx at Giza that depicts the young prince standing before these two deities. It states that he looked after the horses in the stables of his father, the pharaoh, with such zeal that he made Astarte and Reshef rejoice.[3]

"Reshef" is one of many spelling variations for a deity who, like Astarte, was worshipped by his Near Eastern name, but depicted in the Egyptian style. He wears the white Egyptian crown with a gazelle head projecting from it over the forehead. Sometimes he has a Sumerian-style pointed beard. He most often carries a spear or mace. His name can mean "firebrand," "plague-giver," or "ravager" in Hebrew, and he was commonly called upon to combat *Akha*, a demon who caused severe abdominal pain.

Reshef's traditional powers and characteristics make him ideal to invoke in spells aimed at relieving stress and anxiety, since the stomach is the location of the sacral chakra that governs hidden emotions. Confronting, analyzing, and intelligently combatting these emotions will stop them from creating disease.

# SPELL FOR RELIEVING
# STRESS AND ANXIETY

The following spell can be used to relieve stress, anxiety, and PTSD (Post Traumatic Stress Disorder), and to focus healing energies on the sacral chakra for humans and animals alike. You can also use it to protect stables or any home where a horse or pet resides.

***What you need:***
Calendula oil.

***Instructions:***
First, invoke the great Reshef, using these words:

> *Great Reshef, stop all intruders!*
>
> *Great Reshef, oh thou who art revered by the spirits of horses past and present, stop the demons that would cause [my/ my horse's/my pet's] anxiety and seek to lodge in [my/my horse's/my pet's] stomach! For it was thy might that protected the horses in the stables of the pharaoh against colic and maltreatment.*
>
> *I call on thine energy to cleanse and purify my sacral chakra.*
>
> *I call on thine energy to cleanse and purify the sacral chakra of my beloved [pet's/horse's name].*
>
> *And I call on thine energy to cleanse, purify, and protect the stables and the abode of my beloved [pet's/horse's name] from all evil, negativity, obsessions, and especially all enemies.*
>
> *My sacrifice to thee, great Reshef, is trust. As the great pharaohs trusted thine integrity, so dost thou have my word in heart and spirit that I trust in thee without fail. For never was it known that someone who called on thee was left unanswered.*

*I give thee permission, great god, to enter my sacred and holy*
*place, that area within me that needs to be purged of anger,*
*betrayal, fear, and even hatred. Do thou the same for my*
*beloved [pet's/horse's name].*

Slowly rub calendula oil in a clockwise motion on your sacral
chakra, which is located approximately two to three inches below
the navel. Then say:

*Great Reshef, bring light and healing energy where there is none.*

*Great Reshef, protect me with a father's love.*

*And do thou bless my spirit, so I may bring comfort to my*
*loved ones and to [pet's/horse's name].*

Stop rubbing the calendula oil on your sacral chakra. While the
energy is still running through your hands, extend them in prayer,
palms open and facing downward (the Benedictine pose) over
your pet/horse. Then close the spell by saying:

*Great Reshef, bring thy light and healing energy where there*
*is none.*

*Great Reshef, protect [pet's/horse's name] with thy fatherly love.*

*Great Reshef, bless [pet's/horse's name]'s spirit, so we may*
*both feel thy heavenly healing and peace.*

Why did I choose calendula? Calendula is used to remove
anything that has become stagnant in our lives. It attracts light,
love, and the power necessary to remove anxiety, PTSD, and
obsessions. It captures the energy and warmth of the sun, including the orange hues associated with the sacral chakra. Because of
this, it can be called upon to bring nurturing opportunities into
the auric field and into the physical body.

## ADDITIONAL RESOURCES

### Primary sources

Gardner, John, and John Maier, trans. *Gilgamesh* (New York: Vintage Books, 1984).

Kammenhuber, A. *Hippologia hethitica* (Wiesbaden, Germany: Harrassowitz, 1961). The Kikkuli text has yet to be translated into English, but is available here in its entirety in German.

Lichtheim, Miriam. *Ancient Egyptian Literature*, vol. 2 (Berkeley, CA: University of California Press, 1976).

Sandars, N. K., trans. *Poems of Heaven and Hell from Ancient Mesopotamia* (London: Penguin Books, 1971).

### Secondary sources

Anthony, David W. *The Horse, the Wheel, and Language: How Bronze-Age Riders from the European Steppes Shaped the Modern World* (Princeton, NJ: Princeton University Press, 2010).

—————. "Horses, ancient Near East and Pharaonic Egypt." In Roger S. Bagnall, et al., ed. *The Encyclopedia of Ancient History* (Chichester, England: Blackwell Publishing Ltd., 2013), pp. 3311–3314.

Collins, Billie Jean, ed. *A History of the Animal World in the Ancient Near East* (Leiden, Netherlands: Brill, 2001).

Dawson, Tess. *The Horned Altar: Rediscovering and Rekindling Canaanite Magick* (Woodbury, MN: Llewellyn Publications, 2013).

Drews, Robert. *Early Riders: The Beginnings of Mounted Warfare in Asia and Europe* (New York: Routledge Press, 2004).

King, Leonard W. *Babylonian Magic and Sorcery* (York Beach, ME: Weiser, 2000; reprint of 1896).

Lenormant, François. *Chaldean Magic: Its Origin and Development* (York Beach, ME: Weiser, 1999; reprint of 1878).

Meeks, Dimitri. "L'introduction du cheval en Égypte et son insertion dans les croyances religieuses." In Armelle Gardeisen, ed., *Les équidés dans le monde méditerranéen antique* (Lattes, France: CNRS, 2005), pp. 51–59.

Outram, Alan K., et al. "The Earliest Horse Harnessing and Milking," *Science* 323 (March 2009), pp. 1332–1335.

Raulwing, Peter, ed. and trans. *The Kikkuli Text. Hittite Training Instructions for Chariot Horses in the Second Half of the 2nd Millennium B.C. and Their Interdisciplinary Context* (text published directly online, 2009). Retrieved from *http://www.lrgaf.org* (accessed 9/26/2019).

Recht, Laerke, "Asses Were Buried with Him: Equids as Markers of Sacred Space in the Third and Second Millennia BC in the Eastern Mediterranean." In Louis Daniel Nebelsick, et al., ed., *Sacred Space: Contributions to the Archaeology of Belief* (Archaeologica Hereditas, 13) (Warsaw, Poland: Institute of Archaeology, Cardinal Stefan Wyszyń ski University, 2018), pp. 65–94.

Watanabe, Chikako E. *Animal Symbolism in Mesopotamia: A Contextual Approach* (Vienna: Universität Wien Institut für Orientalistik, 2002).

Zivie-Coche, Christiane. "Foreign Deities in Egypt." In Jacco Dieleman and Willeke Wendrich, eds., *UCLA Encyclopedia of Egyptology* (Los Angeles, 2011).

**NOTES**

1 Outram, 2009, and Anthony, 2010.
2 Raulwing, 2009.
3 Tablet VI, column I, lines 10, 20.
4 Tablet VI, column II, lines 53–56.
5 Lichtheim, 1976, vol. 2, p. 42.

# Chapter 4

# THE AFRICAN RIVER HORSE

The unpredictably violent and massive hippopotamus, whose name derives from the Greek for "horse of the river," was feared and revered in ancient Egypt as much as she is today among the Kalabari of Nigeria. Taweret and Ammit, two hippopotamus deities from the ancient Egyptian pantheon, played roles in rituals surrounding birth and death, while, southwest of Egypt, the mask of the hippo water spirit Otobo was used as part of a ritual ceremony.

## Taweret and Ammit

Both Taweret and Ammit are hybrid creatures whose bodies are part hippo, part crocodile, and part lion—the most dangerous beasts known in Egyptian culture. Taweret, known as the Lady of the Pure Waters, was the fierce goddess of fertility and childbirth. She appears as a pregnant hippo standing upright with sagging breasts. She has the back of a crocodile and the claws of a lioness, and her paws rest on the hieroglyph *sa*, which means "protection." The Egyptians were keen observers of nature, and Taweret's savagery reflects the very real strength of the bond between a mother hippo and her calf. In fact, bow-shaped knives fashioned out of the hippo's long canines and inscribed with prayers were key tools in ceremonies to protect children and pregnant women from danger. Sometimes this goddess appears in tomb frescos in which she is meant to assist with rebirth into the next life.

Ammit, the Devourer of the Dead and the Eater of Hearts, was a funerary deity. The Egyptians believed that the heart was the center of intelligence where what we would call the soul resided. In fact, the brain was removed via the nostrils during the embalming procedure and discarded. Ammit appears regularly in painted scrolls with the spells from the so-called *Book of the Dead*. During the judgment process, the goddess of justice, Maat, supervised the weighing of the heart on her great scales against the symbol of purity, an ostrich feather. Souls she found unworthy were deprived of an afterlife in the presence of the god Osiris. Instead, Ammit, who presided over a lake of fire, devoured these unworthy souls and condemned them to a second death as homeless, restless spirits. All this makes Ammit an ideal deity to petition to rebuke a psychic attack.

# SPELL TO REBUKE A PSYCHIC ATTACK

Sometimes brevity in a spell can be misleading. If meant to succeed, any spell said with true, clear intent and with an impassioned plea—starting in the center of the gut, spiraling up through the heart, and then sent hurtling out to the gods and goddesses—will be granted. Do not be afraid of your power. Use it to protect yourself from your enemies, psychic attacks, rage and jealousy, and to exact righteous revenge.

***What you need:***
One black candle.

***Instructions:***
To begin, light the black candle. Then say this spell once with power and conviction:

*Taweret, Lady of the Pure Waters, come to my aid, for I am unjustly attacked.*

*Ammit, Eater of the Evil Heart, come to my aid; I seek righteous revenge.*

*SA! SA! SA! SA! I invoke ye, wise and powerful forces. Work for me now.*

*My enemies challenge my power and strike while I am weak.*

*Jealousy and rage run through them. But I am blameless.*

*SA! SA! SA! SA! I invoke ye, wise and powerful forces. Judge my enemies now.*

*Taweret, Lady of the Pure Waters, may I always be worthy of your blessings.*

*Ammit, Eater of the Evil Heart, may my heart remain true and escape your wrath.*

*SA! SA! SA! SA! I thank ye, wise and powerful forces. All evil has been removed.*

Why did I choose a black candle? By lighting the black candle, you symbolically burn away all it represents. In this case, the black candle represents evil and all negative forces working against you.

## Otobo

To the southwest of Egypt lies the Niger River delta, the largest in Africa, measuring 27,000 square miles. This dense network of rivers, streams, and mangrove swamps is home to the hippo. The religion of two groups of the people who live there, the Kalabari Ijaw and Igbo, centers on ancestor veneration and the belief in water spirits called *owuamapu*. The physical environment of these cultures is reflected in their vision of the spiritual world, so, for them, a great body of water separates the land of the living from the land of the dead. The owuamapu share their watery dwellings with the spirits of unborn humans as well as with ancestors.

The Ijaw practice a type of divination known as *igbadai*, which entails questioning the dead to surmise if they have lived a good life and how they passed away. To preserve a healthy balance between the living and the dead, the Ijaw celebrate in honor of their dead once a year. The ritual festivities include a masquerade in which dancers are accompanied by drumming. The man who dons the hippopotamus mask of the water spirit Otobo—which features large tusk-like protrusions—takes on the qualities of the animal while he dances, threatening both the audience and other dancers. It is not uncommon for the owuamapu to possess him, so it makes sense that Otobo was often invoked to establish contact with the dead.

## SPELL FOR ANCESTRAL SCRYING

The Ijaw ceremony described above accumulated great amounts of energy through ritual, tradition, and spirit possession. To this day, it still holds power. Use this spell to dip into its energies to contact your own ancestors and spirit guides, and to receive an important message from them.

***What you need:***
Black ink and a small, shallow receptacle approximately four to six inches in diameter in which to mix the ink and water. I suggest ceramic, plastic, stone, or glass, because the black ink may stain. Otherwise, choose a vessel that you can discard. You will also need some African drumming music.

***Instructions:***
Fill the bowl three-quarters full with water and add five to six drops of black ink. Stir with something disposable like a straw or piece of wood until the ink is fully blended. Place the bowl on a flat surface. Turn on the drumming music and sit quietly in front of your scrying bowl. Consciously center yourself by taking

several deep breaths. Use self-talk to focus, telling your physical body to relax and your mind to stay alert. Breathe normally. Chant the spell below three, six, or nine times:

> *Otobo, protect me, Otobo, guide me;*
>
> *I peer into the sacred waters of the ethers.*
>
> *Otobo, protect me, Otobo, guide me;*
>
> *Call forth my ancestors and spirit guides.*
>
> *Otobo, protect me, Otobo, guide me;*
>
> *Bring me a life-changing message.*

Now focus your gaze on the black water. Ask the spirits of the water (known as undines, or in this case, owuamapu) to give you an important message from a deceased ancestor. Try to keep your mind blank. If a thought comes, let it. Then let it go. Remain still and relaxed as you wait to see your message in the blackness of the water.

## ADDITIONAL RESOURCES

For a facsimile and translation of one version of *The Book of the Dead* in the papyrus of Ani, see Raymond Faulkner, trans. *The Egyptian Book of the Dead: The Book of Going Forth by Day* (San Francisco: Chronicle Books, 1994).

For information on *The Book of the Dead of Hunefer*, 19th Dynasty (London: British Museum, EA9901,3) and an image of the famous judgment scene, see *http://britishmuseum.org*.

For an example of an Otobo mask, see Eskenazi Museum of Art at Indiana University: *http://iub.edu*.

For a three-dimensional, printable Otobo mask, see the British Museum's site: *https://myminifactory.com*.

### Secondary sources

Barley, Nigel. *Nigerian Arts Revisited* (Paris: Somogy Art Publishers, 2016).

Cole, Herbert M. *Igbo: Visions of Africa Series* (Milan, Italy: 5 Continents Editions, 2013).

——————. *Invention and Tradition: The Art of Southeast Nigeria* (Munich, Germany: Prestel Verlag, 2012).

# Chapter 5

# THE MARBLE HORSE

Horse magick was always strong and deep, and, in the end, loud and victorious. And it has withstood the test of time for over two millennia. When Poseidon, god of the ocean, and Athena, goddess of wisdom, fought to be the patron of a key port city in Attica, they each offered a gift to the city's first ruler, Cecrops, and its citizens. Poseidon raised his trident and struck the face of the flat-topped, massive hill that dominates the cityscape, known as the *akropolis* (literally, "the place high above the city"). Cracks radiated out from the point of contact and the ground shook. Salt water gushed forth in a plume and filled a well, also revealing a brilliant, white horse, the first of its kind. In this manner, Poseidon demonstrated his power over the sea as well as the land.

Athena, unperturbed, held her spear aloft, point down, and let it drop, leaving a chink in the marble on which she stood. She leaned over and touched it and a brilliant green shoot rose from the stone, and then another, and another. They began intertwining and rapidly grew in height and width. Bark encased a gnarled trunk and a canopy of branches created shade, as deep green leaves shot through with silver sprouted on them. In the twinkling of an eye, the boughs were heavily weighed down with a hitherto unknown fruit. And the citizens marveled at Athena's gift—the olive. The fruit was destined to make them hale and wealthy; it became a staple in their diet and its oil became a lucrative export. Because of this, the city pledged itself forever to Athena and bears her name to this day—Athens. Poseidon vanished in haste, but the event was recorded in stone.

The Athenians enshrined these sacred points of heavenly contact with the earth by building a multichambered temple there, known as the *Erechtheum,* to safeguard Poseidon's well and Athena's olive tree. Much of this story has been forgotten and today the temple is, perhaps, most renowned for its balcony, which has columns in the form of maidens, properly referred to as *caryatids.*

# The Parthenon

The Akropolis, even in ruins, holds traces of the magickal bond between the horse and the ancient Greeks. On it sits a lavish temple devoted to Athena, which is called the Parthenon (*parthenos* refers to Athena as a "virgin"). The temple was built between 447 and 438 BCE. One of its most distinguishing features is its sculpture, the work of Pheidias (c. 480–430 BCE), and there are literally hundreds of horses on this monument.[1]

On the exterior of the Parthenon, horses appear on the pediments. These triangular, gabled spaces rest on the columns at the east and west (short) ends of the rectangular building, and their sculptural content tells mythic tales on a monumental scale. The east facade, the entrance, depicts the birth of Athena, who emerged fully grown from the head of Zeus. On it, the horses of Helios, god of the sun, and Selene, goddess of the moon, are ingeniously situated in the left and right corners, as if the steeds are rising and descending, respectively. They provide a sense of heavenly rhythm in which the cycle of day and night is forever in motion. Helios' horses emerge eagerly, lifting their heads and snorting, to pull his chariot. Their ears are pricked up at attention and they have upraised hooves. At the other end of the pediment, the head of one of Selene's horses literally hangs over the edge of the sculptural frame with its muzzle open in exhaustion, blood pumping in bulging veins and nostrils dilated, having worked hard for its mistress throughout the night.

The other group of horses on the Parthenon is completely visible only to those who walk in its colonnade. This sculptural section most likely immortalizes a civic, religious festival held every four years in Athena's honor, the *Panathenaia* (literally "all of Athens"). On one section of the frieze, which runs in two parts down each long side of the Parthenon, a parade with horses commences far below the Akropolis, in the city. One can still imagine their hooves clattering on marble while participants and bystanders sang and cheered.

Just as Prometheus introduced fire to humanity, Athena introduced the horse bridle, thus making it possible to control an otherwise unused source of power. According to most ancient accounts, Athena gave the mythical hero Bellerophon a golden bridle to tame Pegasus. The Parthenon frieze, as described above, is nearly half horses, either pulling chariots or being ridden in strict formation. None of these horses have names, just like the unknown forces of power that lie dormant or semi-dormant within your own temple of the mind, so it is not surprising that you can call on them to help you access those powers, as in the next spell.

## SPELL TO ENTER A TRANCE STATE

To give more depth to this spell, I suggest that you choose an "unknown" horse from the Parthenon frieze and make it your own through creative visualization. If you need help bringing up a visual image, you can find an excellent representation of the freize at *https://en.wikipedia.org*. Once you have chosen a horse, give your "unknown" a name. Give it wings, assign it a breed, make it your own—as if it had already sprung forth from within you. You will ride your horse in the creative visualization below, as Bellerophon rode Pegasus, galloping along an earthly path, up into the air, beyond the clouds, and into a trance state. Then, with this imagery intact, you will begin chanting the Spell to Enter a Trance State.

***What you need:***

A comfortable chair, a deep-purple candle, and essential oil of honeysuckle. For optimal results you will need a strong, steady candle flame, so be sure to place your lit candle in an area free from drafts.

***Instructions:***

Burn the honeysuckle oil/fragrance in an oil diffuser or burn honeysuckle incense in stick or cone form (the bark is not suitable for this spell). Light the candle. Place it close enough that you can stare into the flame. Sit comfortably in your favorite chair and enter a relaxed state. Then read this creative visualization:

> *A white stallion standing regal and strong notices your presence. Instantly, there is a connection between you, an understanding of what is to come, your purpose for meeting.*
>
> *You hear:*
>
> *I am the horse unknown, finally known, that you will ride effortlessly. I will grow wings and lift you to a higher plane.*
>
> *You respond:*
>
> *And I am the one who gives thanks for your awakening. I will ride upon your back through this open field, become one with you, and up into the heavens above.*
>
> *Once on the white stallion's back, you notice something different—your horse has grown wings. They are the size of the largest eagle's wing times three. They are kept folded neatly and drape in a compact form from its shoulders, past its flanks, to the tip ends of its haunches. Leaning forward, you are about to stroke your mount's neck and mane, but you embrace it instead. Suddenly, the scent of honeysuckle fills your nose. The stallion's fragrance, as mystical as it should be, still catches you off guard. You close your eyes and allow the stallion to walk.*
>
> *Breathing in deeply, tightening your embrace, the left side of your face pressed against the stallion's soft coat, your hands*

*caress him in long, slow strokes. You follow the hypnagogic
images forming behind your closed eyelids. Now you match the
stallion's frequency and you are one with the unknown that is
now known. You are the winged horse. And you begin to pick
up your pace. You are trotting.*

*Mother Earth offers you the gift of an immense field of dark
earth, cool and dry beneath you. It is a perfectly steady foundation, and you never falter. Its only purpose is to serve you
and keep you. Thank you, Mother Earth.*

*You snort and break into a canter at the feeling of security
beneath your hooves. Steady and balanced, you take the lead
with your right hoof, running three beats to the gait. Wind
cools your muscles and you fall more deeply into union and go
faster. Now a thirst to move even more quickly takes over. You
are ready. Gallop! You are galloping!*

*You stretch your wings away from your haunches, from your
flanks, out straight, perpendicular to your shoulders. They force
the air downward and you catch the lift. You take flight.*

*No more sound of hooves on ground. Just peace, a whisper of
white noise, and the slow, limitless, rhythmic pulsing of the
hypnagogic images.*

You are now in a trance state and ready to perform the spell.

The trick is to begin chanting the spell in a rhythmic manner
(commit it to memory or record it and keep it playing on a loop)
while staring intently at the flame of the candle. Keep in mind
that the goal here is not to "see" a vision in the flame, but to keep
your mind calm and focused so you can enter a trance state. Close
your eyes and continue chanting the spell below:

*The chant to trance*

*From stance to dance*

*First start to walk*

*Then trot, don't stop.*

*Next canter, get faster.*

*Now, galloping free;*

*Emotion, slow motion,*

*Rhythm in me.*

*Thought-less, free flowing;*

*Relaxed with not knowing.*

*Take astral landscape*

*Enough to escape*

*Time.*

Now read through and imagine the creative visualization again. Finally, with your eyes shut, continue to chant the spell as long as possible in the same rhythmic manner, while trying to keep your mind empty of thoughts. Paying attention to the hypnagogic images will help keep your mind clear. Their kaleidoscopic movement focuses your attention away from distracting thoughts.

Why did I design my spell in counterpoint rhythm? Counterpoint rhythm, another term for syncopation, places the accent on words that you wouldn't normally accentuate. In this case, I create a sense of a building momentum followed by a hard stop, not unlike the technique used by the sculptor(s) who created the multitude of superimposed and staggered horses on the Parthenon frieze. This also helps you commit the spell to memory more easily. Most important, it can help to lull you into an alpha state.

The best way to manifest results from magick is by entering an altered state, preferably an alpha state. You may enter an alpha state, sometimes known as a "twilight state," just before you fall asleep. For this to happen, however, your body must be asleep and your mind still awake—simultaneously. These two affirmations may help you train your mind to enter an alpha state more readily. Say them prior to meditation or spellwork:

*Physical body, relax and go to sleep!*

*Mind, stay awake!*

Why did I choose the color purple and the essential oil or fragrance of honeysuckle? Deep purple is one of the colors easily seen in hypnagogic imagery. Honeysuckle is used to induce astral sight.

## Helios and Pyrois

Immortal horses pull Helios' chariot with an indomitable force. Do they know that they are immortal? If they do, they've accepted a sacred function—to display the glory of the sun for all time. Their desire to pull the chariot of Helios for eternity parallels the blind force within humanity, and specifically those who are incarnated, to obtain fame and recognition or who feel they merit it.

Two diminutive men in history made themselves giants through willpower and artful advertising. Alexander the Great had himself deified in Egypt as a sun god, as he is depicted on ancient Greek coins. His force burned so brightly that he expanded his empire from the small province of Macedonia to the edges of the known world. And what of Louis XIV of France, *le Roi Soleil* (the Sun King)? He had himself depicted as Apollo, sometimes behind the chariot of the sun, throughout the fountains and gardens of his château at Versailles. His genius was powerful enough to manipulate the Parisian aristocracy to move the royal capital itself. He burned an indelible mark in history.

This power is not limited to kings, however, for we are all spiritual royalty. The spell below will help you allow Helios and his fiery horse, Pyrois, to awaken in you.

## SPELL FOR FAME AND RECOGNITION

This spell can help to arouse your own indomitable force and ambition. Let your yearning for life challenge you to leave behind a second sun around which the earth can orbit!

## What you need:

One carnelian, one rough opal (a fragment or small vein of opal in matrix will do just fine), one natural citrine (not irradiated/heat-treated amethyst), essential oil of cinnamon or cinnamon incense, and one gold or deep-yellow candle.

## Instructions:

On an altar facing east, light the incense or burn the essential oil of cinnamon in an oil diffuser. This is your offering to the solar deity, Helios, and his steed, Pyrois, whose name means "the fiery one." (His other three steeds are named Aithos, Bronte, and Euos.) Light the gold or deep-yellow candle. Hold the three crystals in your left hand and make a fist. Take your right hand and place it over your left hand. Raise them both to your solar plexus chakra. Face east (facing your altar) and close your eyes. Conjure a feeling of intense, fiery purpose. Say these words to the spirit of Pyrois:

> *Vanquisher of night, supernatural fire,*
>
> *Unleash your force within me, do not tire.*

Now open your eyes and turn 180° clockwise (to your right). You should now be facing west, and your altar should be directly behind you. In this way, you have symbolically awakened the spirit of Pyrois within you and have symbolically traveled his path—raising the sun and journeying from east to west. Turn to your right another 180° clockwise, finishing the circle. You should be facing your altar and the cardinal point east.

Place the crystals on your altar to the right of the candle. While standing, with your eyes closed or open, say the following spell six times (not five, not seven, but six):

> *Oh, Helios, oath-maker, I invoke thee,*
>
> *Thou who holdest the reins of Pyrois,*
>
> *That horse of pure fire and indomitable force,*
>
> *Make room in thy chariot for me.*
>
> *This pact I make for thee to endorse;*

*Together, not alone, let us rise and become the sun.*

*Do not let our names be forgotten;*

*Not thine, not mine, not that of Pyrois.*

*Do not let them be erased,*

*For that is my task I wholly take up,*

*A pact, an oath, between us three.*

*I swear on my soul; I brand it in fire;*

*And as my will, so mote it be.*

Let the candle burn out naturally. Collect your crystals and keep them in a place in your bedroom where you can see them.

For maximum results, work this spell on six consecutive full moons or during a waxing moon in the astrological sign of Leo. You can also replace cinnamon incense with the resin storax.

Who is Pyrois and how can his magick help us obtain fame and recognition? Pyrois pulls the chariot of Helios, the sun God, with all his force until his job is complete, when the day is done. This intensely spirited horse will work until you reach your goal—as long as you work just as hard and keep your promise to raise up his name, along with Helios, as you reach the top and raise your own!

Helios is known as the oath-maker, so please do not work this spell without proper respect. Do not make a promise if you cannot keep it. In magick, I call that playing with fire. Helios and Pyrois are archetypes. Helios, as the sun, the center of our solar system, bestows light on and sustains our planet. He determines whether life continues. He creates the seasons and the beauty of a sunrise, the signal of dawn. Pyrois represents indomitable strength and unstoppable willpower. Helios controls this blind force with his reins (a secret symbol for our central nervous system). This is power of such a high degree that it can change your destiny—without concern for consequences. It is pure, distilled dynamism.

Why must the spell be recited six times? Six is the number corresponding to the sun in the Practical Qabalah and on the glyph of the Tree of Life.

Why did I choose cinnamon and/or storax? Both cinnamon and storax (a resin from the trunk of *Liquidambar orientalis*) attract solar energies. Cinnamon is also associated with prosperity and good luck. Storax can be burned for protection.

Why did I choose a gold or deep-yellow candle? Both colors represent the sun and solar deities. Gold and yellow are also associated with the solar (sun) plexus chakra, and with good luck, prosperity, positive energy, and recognition.

Why did I choose carnelian, natural citrine, and rough opal? Carnelian is associated with fire and passion. Its properties align with Pyrois and can attract and enhance his energies within you. Natural citrine is associated with the sun, solar energies, and protection. Its properties align with Helios and can attract and enhance his energies with you as well. Rough opal is associated with Mercury, speed, and power. Its properties, when used in conjunction with carnelian and natural citrine, will quicken your magick.

## Selene and the Moon Chariot

Selene, the Titan goddess of the moon, was, according to most accounts, the daughter of Hyperion and Theia. She was thus the sister of Helios and Eos, the goddess of dawn. Winged horses drew Selene's chariot across the night sky, driven by the goddess wearing a crown bearing the moon in its various phases. Some called her Phoebe and said she had wings; others claimed that she had oxen horns on her head, reminiscent of Isis.

In an interesting example of magickal synchronicity, the crescent moon headdress and the crystal ball or sphere can both be considered reflections of two of the Hindu *tattwas* or *Tattvas*—geometric shapes in Hindu philosophy that represent each of the elements: earth, fire, water, air, spirit—specifically *apas*, representing water, and *vayu*, representing air. When the circular vayu sits within the crescent cradle of apas, they combine to create focus and concentration, two key elements in magick. Use them to enhance your magickal skills and to create your own destiny in your crystal ball with a little help from Selene and her gleaming, silvery horses.

## SPELL TO CREATE YOUR OWN DESTINY

Before you begin this spell, you need to understand the difference between a vision and a thought. A vision is not a self-construct—it does not originate in your mind. You are not its author. When a vision occurs (if you are not clairvoyant or used to having visions), you will be in a state of wonderment because it is an unexpected arrival. A loud noise or any distraction can interrupt a train of thought, whereas a vision will come to you in the twinkling of an eye, no matter where you may be, no matter what you may be doing. A vision will affirm itself by manifesting in the physical realm. In other words, it will happen. Or, as the ancients say: As above, so below.

Visions are not hallucinations. Hallucinations do not manifest naturally. They are the result of external stimulation and can also derive from mental illness or any number of pathologies. But no external stimulants—no drugs or mind-altering substances—are necessary for a vision to occur.

A thought, however, is, for the most part, something you actively construct and create with your mind. It is a notion or idea. We have so many thoughts during our conscious hours that we have become accustomed to receiving them—unlike visions, which can startle you.

There are two necessary elements for this spell to work properly: a point of inspiration and a well-formed thought based on your inspiration. For example: You find yourself watching two lovers holding hands as they walk down the street. Conflicting feelings of resentment, jealousy, happiness, warmth, loneliness, and love compete for your attention. You, my friend, have just been inspired.

Acting on that inspiration, you decide to try this spell in order to create your own destiny. A thought begins to form that would otherwise have remained dormant. Searching for the ideal mate now appeals to you. You conjure up romantic images of standing in front of the famous Trevi fountain in Rome with this person. You take it a step further and imagine that you are both wearing wedding rings. Now you are ready.

### What you need:

One silver candle, one moonstone, and one crystal ball (clear quartz or leaded glass).

### Instructions:

Create a well-formed thought based on your point of inspiration. Write it out in simple, everyday terms if you feel this will help. No poetry or classical literature is necessary. If you've been journaling or keeping a diary, that's a great place to start. Next, sit comfortably holding a moonstone (it can be palm-sized; tumbled or rough; white, peach, black, or rainbow). Place your crystal ball and lit silver candle on a table, ideally an altar.

Project your thought into the center of the crystal ball. Ask Selene to hold the thought for you. It's difficult for most people to hold a thought with clarity for more than several moments. With this spell, you're in luck. Selene herself will hold your thought in her bosom even as you sleep. Place your trust in her with this matter, for she is benevolent, wise, and ever watchful. Even as her steeds carry her moon chariot across the night sky, she will collect all your thoughts and forgotten dreams with a scoop of her hand only to return them as metaphorical nourishment in the morning.

Once you have projected your thought into the center of the crystal ball, recite this spell at least nine times:

*By the time I spend time on holding this thought,*

*I will have remembered what you will have not.*

*Oh! Eye in the sky, permit me to try,*

*Like your horses that fly both distant and nigh.*

*Carry my wish from star to star;*

*Bring into my hands what once was afar.*

*May moon drops form in a silvery cup;*

*I lift it now and drink them all up.*

Don't underestimate the powers of the moon. Remember the eagerness with which you began, and when you're ready to give up—don't! Selene just may surprise you!

Why did I choose a moonstone? In ancient Greek lore, the moonstone is associated with Selene.[2] In the 5th-century-BCE Greek epic tale of Dionysus, the author Nonnus writes of Selene's pure white stone, which waxes and wanes as the moon purifies her liquid light and milks out the fire of the sun.[3] Nonnus also emphasizes that Selene's stone makes men full of desire.[4]

Why did I choose a crystal ball? Crystal balls are divinatory tools that help focus thoughts. They are what you use to see a vision. So why not project your own inspirational thought into this spiritual vessel?

Why did I choose a silver candle? The color silver, as well as the metal, is associated with the moon.

Why must you recite the spell at least nine times? Nine is the number corresponding to the moon in the Practical Qabalah and on the glyph of the Tree of Life.

### ADDITIONAL RESOURCES

The Panathenaic Festival Frieze on the Parthenon is enormous! If you wish to do Athena justice, you will study it carefully on the websites of the British Museum, where much of the sculpture is now located, and of the Acropolis Museum in Athens, where you will find stunning recreations of the sculpture with its original paint, gilding, and trappings. See *https://britishmuseum.org* and *https://theacropolismuseum.gr.*

The original text of Nonnus' *Dionysiaca* is available in English translation in full at: *http://theoi.com.*

### Secondary sources

The traditional interpretation of the Parthenon's frieze as the Panathenaia does not stand alone. For a range of opposing schools of thought, see, for example:

Burkert, Walter. *Greek Religion*, trans. John Raffan (Cambridge, MA: Basil Blackwell Publisher and Harvard University Press, 1985).

Condos, Theony. *Star Myths of the Greeks and Romans: A Sourcebook* (Grand Rapids, MI: Phanes Press, 1997).

Connelly, Joan Breton. *The Parthenon Enigma* (New York: Alfred A. Knopf, 2014).

Jenkins, Ian. *The Parthenon Frieze* (Austin, TX: University of Texas Press, 1994).

——————. *The Parthenon Sculptures* (Cambridge, MA: Harvard University Press, 2007).

Neils, Jennifer. *Goddess and Polis: The Panathenaic Festival in Ancient Athens* (Princeton, NJ: Princeton University Press, 1992).

——————, ed. *The Parthenon: From Antiquity to the Present* (Cambridge, England: Cambridge University Press, 2005).

### NOTES

1 On his involvement with this project, Plutarch, Life of Pericles,
13.4–9.
2 Nonnus, Dionysiaca.
3 Ibid., 5. 88.
4 Ibid., 32. 22.

*Chapter 6*

# THE WET HORSE

Horses are no strangers to water. Herds running on a beach provide stock shots for artists and filmmakers trying to symbolize freedom and embody romanticism. Their movement creates a breathtaking spectacle of rippling reflections, water splashing under hooves, and slick manes and tails waving about in the wind. Feral horses and ponies on Chincoteague and Assateague Islands (in Virginia and Maryland) and the wild Camargue horses—perhaps one of the most ancient breeds, now found in the Rhône delta in southern France—have even learned to thrive in swampy marshes and eat seaweed. But in the realm of magick, the relationships between mythical, mystical, and divine horses and bodies of water are varied and unexpected.

## Poseidon and Amphitrite

Poseidon, the Olympian god of the sea, is a deity of profound power, one to be taken seriously. The ancient Greek poet Homer addressed him as the great "shaker of the earth, tamer of horses . . . and savior of ships."[1] His reputed powers have inspired artists in all media, across millennia. One has but to recall the scene in the film *The Fellowship of the Ring* in which the elven princess, Arwen, temporarily vanquishes the black-clad wraith riders by conjuring a herd of watery horses to plunge them into treacherous rapids. Although Homer's chapter on Poseidon follows that of Athena in this book, Poseidon is, in fact, both older and more powerful than she. His dominion encompasses all the waters and the ever-moving sea, and is second only to that of heaven. His waters have flooded the earth, drowned many a human, and swallowed countless seafaring vessels. To placate him, the Greeks offered many of his favorite sacrifices, including bellowing bulls and horse-drawn chariots.

The ancients, for whom maritime trade was a critical part of many economies, were wise to worship Poseidon and did so with great respect and reverence. The Greeks erected massive temples devoted to him, temples that commanded panoramic views on the furthest edges of the fingerlike promontories of the Peloponnese peninsula. The massive temple at Sounion, built by Perikles as part of a building campaign that included the Parthenon, and the temple at Tainaron on the Mani peninsula are examples of these. Sailors prayed in awed reaction to the cliff-temple at Sounion when they saw it from great distances, either returning to port or passing by. Waves crash high there to this day. Perhaps it was the glint of the setting sun or sacrificial flames on the gilded bronze trident of a monumental statue of Poseidon that reminded them of home or the safety of land. It is said that the temple at Tainaron was once to have been part of a sacred grove near the mouth of a cave that served as a sanctuary for soldiers and, in Roman times, for slaves. The cave was reputed to be an entrance—maybe even *the* entrance—to Hades and probably boasted a statue of Poseidon.

And we must not forget the importance of Amphitrite, Poseidon's wife. The daughter of Oceanus and Tethys, she is both a nereid and oceanid (nymphs associated with the sea). Some have argued that Amphitrite once held a more prominent position as a sea goddess or queen. She also appears in ancient images with a trident, as she does driving the god's chariot behind him on the west pediment of the Parthenon—her customary role. Let us, therefore, celebrate her in the tradition of all feminine deities linked to the sea, like the Great Amma. We can easily envision

her windswept, dressed in fluttering seaweeds in varying trans-
lucent shades of jade to deep green, as cobalt hippocamps draw
her spikey-shell chariot across the noisy sea and heaving waves.
She holds aloft a golden trident and sits in splendor upon a red
coral throne.

In Homer's *Iliad*, Book 13, Poseidon the Earth-shaker makes
a brilliant, resplendent, and fearful appearance. From a vantage
point high above the sea, he looks upon the ships of his beloved
Achaians, who are at the mercy of the Trojans. Moved with pity
and filled with rage, he bounds from land and descends to his
glittering palace in the depths of the sea. He clads himself in
gold and harnesses a pair of bronze-hoofed, wing-swift horses
with fluttering manes of gold to a chariot. He then rises out of
the sea and races over the waves. Although there were appar-
ently eight steeds, only two of their names have come down to
us—Skylla and Sthenios. One Roman writer called these wet
horses "stormy-footed" *ketea* or "sea beasts." (In Biblical Greek,
the word means "whale"; think of *cet*aceans).

Homer's passage hints at something magickal, however. He
lends an air of festivity and joyfulness to his narrative when
he relates that the creatures of the sea come forth in delight
to accompany Poseidon. Tritons (a type of brawny mermen)
sound conch shells and nereid sea maidens flank their lord with
dolphins crowding around.[2] Homer adds that the sea acqui-
esces to Poseidon, parting to permit the deity's chariot to speed
so rapidly that its axle does not even get wet. The god was, in
Homer's imagination, being drawn by hippocamps (literally,
"crooked horses" in ancient Greek)—creatures that have the
front part of a horse and the rear of a fish—who raise the chariot
above the water. These steeds have webbed hooves, membranous
manes, and curling scaly bodies that end in fanning split-fin tails.
The ancients believed they were adult seahorses.

Hippocamps are numerous, social creatures that are as moody
as the seas they inhabit. Although Poseidon and Amphitrite use

them to draw their chariots, they remain free until called upon and lead lives of their own. Waves, currents, tides, salt, silt, sand, and shells—these are the forces and materials with which they work their magick.

Some say the sea holds countless mysteries. In fact, few know that the hippocamps' magick manifests in skyscraper waves that occur under the water. These are hundreds of feet higher than waves that crest above the sea and thousands of times more powerful. Your reputation is like these underwater waves. It has a life of its own and, inconspicuous to all, controls what happens on the surface. Your reputation can transport you throughout your life, building in momentum, or crush you in this life and beyond. In the end, its movement dictates your legacy.

# SPELL TO RESTORE OR DESTROY A REPUTATION

Hippocamps, moving full speed ahead, can joyfully raise your reputation to unimaginable heights—or they can destroy it without another thought. In this spell, you will befriend the hippocamps with the help of Poseidon and Amphitrite.

**What you need:**
One dark-blue, shallow bowl, water, salt, one drop of your blood, one seashell, a hammer or mallet, a towel, and your intuition.

**Instructions:**
Once you have gathered everything necessary, follow the directives within the spell. Let your intuition be your guide.

*To get what you need,*

*Deserving or not,*

*Summon the hippocamps*

*Follow what's taught:*

*Pour water, then salt*

*Into a vessel then halt;*

*It must be dark blue*

*To make the spell true.*


*Prick your right thumb,*

*But keep your tongue mum,*

*For a drop of your blood is due.*


*Water awaits, running or still;*

*Hippocamps too demand their fill.*

As the spell dictates, find a body of water, running or still (puddle, river, ocean, etc.) in which to pour the mixture of blood, salt, and water. Do not discard the shell. As you do, say these words:

*Underwater waves*

*From the Luzon Strait,*

*Rise to the surface, my wish now create.*

If it is a reputation you choose to destroy, wrap the shell in a towel and crush it with a mallet or hammer. Throw the bits of shell back to Mother Earth and you are finished. If it is a reputation you choose to restore, carry the shell with you.

Why do you need blood? Compared to other sacrifices, bodily fluids have an aura strong enough to penetrate quickly and directly into the astral realm. The blood allows you to summon the spirits you are using—in this case, hippocamps—and will enable you to persuade them more easily. It will also coax them to bring about your wish.

Why do you need salt? First, because the spell is oceanic in nature and second, because salt is used in magick for banishing and cleansing. Within this spell, you can banish a good reputation or, perhaps, cleanse a tarnished one.

Why do you need a dark-blue vessel? Dark blue represents the element of water, the ocean, and the dark-blue coloration of the hippocamps. In this case, dark blue represents the naturally occurring phenomenon of internal or underwater waves in places of great depths, like the Luzon Straits in the Philippines.

## ADDITIONAL RESOURCES

### Primary sources

Evelyn-White, Hugh G., trans. *Hesiod, Homeric Hymns, Epic Cycle, Homerica* (Cambridge, MA: Harvard University Press; London: William Heinemann Ltd., 1914).

Homer. *The Iliad: A New Prose Translation*, trans. Martin Hammond (London: Penguin Books, 1987).

—————. *The Odyssey*, trans. Walter Shewring (Oxford, England: Oxford University Press, 1980).

Quintus Smyrnaeus. *The Fall of Troy*, trans. A. S. Way (London: William Heinemann, 1913).

### Secondary sources

Conway, D. J. *Magickal Mermaids and Water Creatures: Invoke the Magick of the Waters* (Newburyport, MA: New Page Books, 2005).

Pepper, Elizabeth, and Barbara Stacy. *The Little Book of Magical Creatures*, rev. ed. (Providence, RI: The Witches' Almanac, 2009).

## NOTES

1  Evelyn-White, *Homeric Hymns* (22).
2  Quintus Smyrnaeus, *Fall of Troy*, 5.88ff.

# Chapter 7

# THE WINGED HORSE

The horse was the most important means of transportation until the invention of the automobile. As such, the horse was the springboard for the human imagination to journey into the unknown. In mythology, horses can be death-defying mounts for heroes and heroines, even vehicles for travel in the sky. Pegasus, whose name means "of the spring (or waters)," is the most well-known of the Immortal Horses, an elite group of equines that served the Greek gods. He and the *pegasi* (plural of "pegasus") are distinguished by their wings.

## Pegasus and the Pegasids

Pegasus came from the union of Poseidon and Medusa when the god took the form of a horse and ravished Medusa in Athena's temple. Outraged by this sacrilegious act, Athena focused her wrath on Medusa, whom she turned into a Gorgon with snakes for hair. Medusa was so frightful to behold that any who looked upon her were turned to stone. The Roman poet Ovid tells us that, when the mythic hero Perseus decapitated Medusa, Pegasus sprang forth fully formed from her neck, with blood spattered all over his mane.[1] Poseidon was thus the father of the first winged horse! Athena tamed the stallion and gave him to the hero Bellerophon, who rode him to victory in battle against the monstrous Chimera. But Zeus had his eye on the winged horse and sent a gadfly to bite him as he carried Bellerophon in flight, causing the hero to fall. Pegasus journeyed without his rider to Mount Olympus, where he became Zeus' bearer of thunderbolts and lightning.

Pegasus is also closely associated with the nine Muses. On the day these fair-tressed, violet-eyed maidens in saffron robes began to sing in a competition, all nature was moved to the point that Mount Helikon, where they resided, started to rise heavenward. This posed a problem, however, for it threatened to cause the mountain to reach the height of the gods' residence on Mount Olympus. Poseidon sent Pegasus to put a stop to this. Pegasus halted the growth of the mountain with a strike of his hoof. This caused water to gush forth from the spot, creating Hippocrene (Horse's Fountain), which became a legendary source of inspiration. Tiny nymphs, the Pegasids, immediately took up residence there.

Some say that, when the Muses saw Pegasus arrive in all his splendor, they stopped their singing to rush and admire him. When they saw the fountain, however, they marveled at its beauty, and the waters there became forever intermingled with their legendary powers. They knelt to peer into its clear depths, and the distinctive violet color of their eyes reflected most strongly in it, imbuing the Pegasids, who rose to meet them, with that hue.

To show his gratitude, Zeus eventually honored Pegasus and transformed him into a permanent starry fixture in the night sky. Pegasus is the seventh largest constellation.[2]

## SPELL FOR ASTRAL TRAVEL AND LUCID DREAMING

As a constellation fixed in the heavens, and as a winged horse admired by both Zeus and the Muses, Pegasus becomes the ideal archetype and totem to transport you into cosmic worlds. Use this spell as a petition for astral travel and lucid dreaming.

*What you need:*

A medium-sized bowl, water, nine Chinese star-anise pods, and a rainbow moonstone.

*Instructions:*

Place the rainbow moonstone in the bowl, cover it with the nine star-anise pods, and fill the bowl three-quarters full with fresh water. Recite this spell over it:

> *Pegasus, I call you forth with all my might;*
> *Come visit me in my dreams tonight.*
>
> *Fly me to that sacred place*
> *Where all that's hidden shows its face.*
>
> *Fill me with your astral light;*
> *Gift me with your psychic sight.*
>
> *Shake me, wake me in my dreams;*
> *Fly me through the moon's bright beams.*

When finished, place the bowl under your bed or on your nightstand.

Why did I choose rainbow moonstone, Chinese star-anise pods, and the number nine? Rainbow moonstone is famous for its ability to induce lucid dreams and astral travel, and open the mind's eye. By placing it next to you or under your bed, you are intentionally channeling its positive energies. Even after this spell is finished and you have successfully traveled through the astral realms or had a lucid dream, keeping the rainbow moonstone close to your bed will help develop these skills.

Star-anise pods are used to enhance psychic abilities. They also have a wonderful, penetrating fragrance.

The number nine is associated with the moon in the Practical Qabalah. The moon is associated with psychic ability, astral travel, and lucid dreaming.

## SPELL FOR INSPIRATION

Water elementals in general can be helpful to those seeking insight or to awaken ideas, but the Pegasids in particular can help you find inspiration because of their connection to Pegasus's spring, enchanted by the nine Muses.

**What you need:**
One eight-ounce glass of fresh spring water and one tumbled amethyst.

**Instructions:**
On the night of a full moon, place the amethyst in a glass three-quarters full of room-temperature spring water. Put your left hand over the top of the water glass, then put your right hand over your left. Imagine the light of the full moon pouring down through your head, neck, throat, shoulders, arms, and hands, through your palms and into the water and amethyst. Recite the spell three, six, or nine times:

> Drink from us our water wise
>
> Charmed by nine pairs of violet eyes.
>
> Grow wings, no rules, all paths explore;
>
> Now change the earth forevermore.
>
> Oh! Inspiration my soul can now use
>
> By the powers of every immortal Muse.

Let the water sit for no longer than sixty minutes. Remove the amethyst and drink the water. Imagine your spirit being charmed by Pegasids, whom the nine Muses charmed with their violet eyes. Let them bring you inspiration, ingenious ideas, and magickal enlightenment. Be sure to sleep with a pen and paper next to your bed. They will come to you in your dreams.

Why did I choose an amethyst? Amethysts naturally occur in hues of purple and violet, the color of the Muses' eyes. They are also associated with insight and can help foster a relationship with them.

Why did I choose the night of the full moon? To escape moon-flux and draw down the most powerful lunar energy into the water and amethyst mixture. Besides, Pegasids tend to love the full moon.

Why did I choose fresh spring water at room temperature? Spring water, for obvious reasons: to replicate water from the original spring, Hippocrene. Water is easier to drink at room temperature and passes through the system more quickly. It is also less jarring than if you were to drink it cold, allowing your mind to enter a relaxed state more easily.

### ADDITIONAL RESOURCES

*Primary sources*
Ovid. *Fasti*, 2nd ed., trans. James G. Frazer, rev. G. P. Goold (Cambridge, MA: Harvard University Press, 1931).

### NOTES

1  Ovid, *Fasti,* 3. 449.
2  Condos, pp. 151–155.

*Chapter 8*

# THE HUMBLE HORSE

In 391 CE, the Christian emperor of Rome, Theodosius I (born 347 CE, emperor in the East from 379 to 392 CE, and of the entire empire from 392 to 395 CE), formally banned the worship of Vesta (Greek Hestia), goddess of the hearth and fertility. In doing so, however, he did not silence the thunder-ringing hooves of a stallion racing off to battle. Instead, he halted the muffled thuds of a humble donkey. But we are revoking this edict!

Vesta was one of the first and last "pagan" deities associated with Rome and was central to the city for over 1000 years before Theodosius's arrival. Now, nearly 2000 years later, Vesta's name must once again ring out from the mouths of those calling for protection in their homes and on the road, and for fruitfulness in their wedding beds.

## Vesta's Donkey

The gentle, steadfast donkey was sacred to Vesta. It powered the mills for tens of thousands of bakers across the Roman Empire, and the goddess held this profession, also proper to the home, dear to her heart. During her festival, the Vestalia (June 5 to 17), Vesta temporarily raised the donkey's mundane status and on June 9, her worshippers crowned this creature with garlands made of flowers and pieces of bread. It is no coincidence that many civilizations prized the donkey as a strong pack animal and reliable mount—especially for women, children, and the elderly.

You only need to recall the Ascended Master, Jesus, who chose to ride a donkey rather than a horse into Jerusalem on the day he was hailed king to understand the symbolism this animal held in ancient times.

But Vesta and her priestesses, the Vestal virgins, were far from humble. They formed part of an imperial cult of immense significance that had a major, government-funded temple in Rome. Unlike most other deities, Vesta's iconography is not a person but a flame, as we often see her on Roman coins, sometimes with a phallus in the center.

## SPELL FOR SAFE PASSAGE

This spell calls for a sacrifice—in this case, making bread. It enhances the power of the spell to use something associated with your own home, like your family's traditional bread recipe. Going out of your way to make the bread increases the power of this magick. In fact, the amount of sacrifice you put into the making of your bread is directly proportional to the degree of success the spell will have.

***What you need:***
A bread recipe or a store-bought prepared dough mixture, if you are not inclined to baking, a plate to put the bread on, and three yellow birthday candles.

***Instructions:***
After you've baked the bread, cut a decent portion, put it on a plate, and place three yellow birthday candles in it. Light the one in the middle first, then the one to the right, and finally the one to the left. Chant the following spell three, six, or nine times:

*Kindly, slowly,*

*Round and round;*

*Steady, reliable,*

*Hoof to ground;*

*Gods' and goddesses' chosen mount,*

*Everyone's safety's paramount.*

Let the candles burn out naturally. Throw the bread back to Mother Earth. Share the remaining loaf with loved ones.

Why did I choose yellow candles? Yellow is associated with the sun, equilibrium, health, success, and safety.

Why did I choose three candles? Three is associated with the mind, body, and soul, all of which this spell is geared to protect.

## ADDITIONAL RESOURCES

*Secondary sources*

Beard, Mary, John North, and Simon Price. *Religions of Rome*, vol. 1 (Cambridge, England: Cambridge University Press, 1998).

DiLuzio, Meghan J. *A Place at the Altar: Priestesses in Republican Rome* (Princeton, NJ: Princeton University Press, 2016).

Fraschetti, Augusto. *Roman Women*, trans. Linda Lappin (Chicago: The University of Chicago Press, 2001).

Johnston, Sarah Iles. *Religions of the Ancient World: A Guide* (Cambridge, MA: The Belknap Press of Harvard University Press, 2004).

Shai, Itzhaq, et al. "The Importance of the Donkey as a Pack Animal in the Early Bronze Age Southern Levant: A View from *Tell eṣ-Ṣfil* Gath," *Zeitschrift des Deutschen Palästina-Vereins* 132 (2016), pp. 1–25.

Way, Kenneth C. *Donkeys in the Biblical World: Ceremony and Symbol* (Winona Lake, IN: Eisenbrauns, 2011).

# Chapter 9

# THE LOVER'S HORSE

The horse can represent polar opposites—lust and love, passion and purity. This concept crystallizes in mythological reconstructions of it, for instance, centaurs and unicorns. Neither of these creatures, however, represents a single emotion.

Centaurs, for instance, embody rape and pillaging in most Greek myths—the exception being Chiron (see chapter 15). In the Middle Ages, the contrasting mythological creature is the unicorn, which often represents virginal innocence and purity of intention. Unicorns are always attracted to committment, making them completely different from centaurs, who like to play the field, so to speak. In other words, unicorns are heart-driven; centaurs are libido-driven. You can call on each of these mythological creatures to obtain the type of love you desire. Or call on them both to satisfy the two aspects of human nature necessary for a happy and fulfilling life—sex and love, heart and libido.

## Stallions and Centaurs

The stallion is a key source for equine magick because of his uncontainable libido and pronounced physical power. These are the traits necessary for him to assume the role as progenitor, leader, and protector of the herd. The centaur, a hybrid creature with the torso of a man and the body of a horse, embodies the potency of the equine sex drive in ancient Greek mythology.

In one tale, centaurs attended the wedding feast of the human Lapith king Pirithous and Hippodameia, whose name means "horse tamer." Once the creatures became drunk, they attempted to molest the bride and began raping and carrying off Lapith women and boys. The ensuing fight between human and "beast," called a centauromachy, was used as an analogy for the divide between the Greeks, who made decisions based on reason, and the "barbarian" enemy, who acted irrationally based on passion. Fine sculptures of this subject appear on the Parthenon in Athens. The theme appears elsewhere with frequency as well, often in erotic scenes in which centaurs have gigantic erections—for instance, on painted ceramic vessels used for mixing and serving wine at symposia, ancient Greek dinner parties.

## SPELL FOR HOT SEX

This spell invokes the physical power of the stallion to arouse the passions.

**What you need:**
One blood-red votive candle and essential oil of ginger.

**Instructions:**
Dress the candle with essential oil of ginger. Light it and say the following spell nine times.[1] This spell can also be worked if you do not have a special someone in mind. Simply use the pronouns him or her in place of a name. The spirits will understand your intent.

> *Stallion of raging fire and sex,*
>
> *Lend me your power for this hex;*
>
> *Consume [name of the one you desire] with flames of desire,*
>
> *Pleasures of the flesh and hidden fire.*
>
> *Of least resistance find a way*

*On top of my body [name/pronoun] must stay.*

*Unbridled passion in my bed,*

*As if it were the night we wed.*

Let the candle burn out naturally.

Why did I choose ginger and a red candle? Ginger has long been known for its properties of vitality and sexual stimulation. Red is associated with passion, lust, power, and sex.

# Unicorns

The tale of the unicorn has been told many, many times, but most tellers give it only a spiritual interpretation. Because of this, writers stress the unicorn's symbolic elements of purity and holiness when, in fact, the creature was just as much a symbol of libido. The most famous images of unicorns are preserved in two sets of tapestries—one in Paris and one in New York. (I will discuss those in Paris here.)

Around 1500, a group of highly skilled women in Flanders wove a set of six tapestries depicting a unicorn and a lady. They worked the images with deep-red silk and gold-wrapped thread for a wealthy male client at the royal court in Paris. Five of the panels clearly represent the senses—sight, smell, taste, touch, sound—but the meaning of the sixth remains mysterious. It shows a woman inside a tent that is flanked by a lion and unicorn. She appears to be about to touch a jeweled necklace in a box that bears the motto, *A mon seul désir* ("For my one desire" or "For the thing I desire most"). The consensus is that this tapestry represents a search for pure or spiritual love. This would presumably have enabled the owner and his family to be released from the earthly greed and sensuality embodied by the physical beauty and incredible financial value of the tapestries, and immerse themselves instead in the tapestries' spirituality.

This interpretation of the unicorn myth reaches far back into the early Middle Ages. At that time, there were painted manuscripts called bestiaries that contained pictures of all types of creatures, real and imaginary. Next to each image, there was text that gave its secret meaning. For example, the unicorn was usually shown with its head in the lap of a maiden, because only innocence could attract this rare creature. That is how hunters procured its horn, which was believed to have the power to purify poisonous water, among other miracles. To the medieval mind, this created a parallel to the Virgin Mary, who drew down the Holy Spirit to conceive Christ.

But the unicorn also represents playful, erotic love, and potent masculine libido. Images carved on ivory-encased mirrors and jewelry boxes make this clear. In these examples, the sculptor treats the unicorn's horn as a phallic symbol. There are depictions of beautiful young ladies sliding floral wreaths onto it, a thinly disguised reference to the sexual act. This multifaceted symbolism can be seen in the Tale of the Soothsayer's Oasis.

## The Tale of the Soothsayer's Oasis

Some say—and tapestries show—that once, so far back in time that none might know, an elusive unicorn came out of his hidden world to lay his head with trust in a virgin's lap. But he did not know she was being used as bait, as part of a carefully plotted attack. Hunters sprang out of hiding, viciously killed the defenseless unicorn, and cut off his magickal horn. They left the unicorn's lifeless and bloodied body in the virgin's arms. We will never know if she was complicit in this act.

Others say, however, that this tale is nothing like the truth and is merely a reflection of human braggadocio. By their account, as the unicorn approached the virgin, he was overcome with a sense of dread. Just before he lay his head in her lap, he struck the ground nervously with his hoof. With flared nostrils, he reared and pivoted on his hindquarters. His instincts proved correct and he eluded the hunters, who emerged from the dense undergrowth with swords drawn. The creature fled in terror, all the while realizing he had been betrayed. Breaking into a full gallop, he left the forest far behind.

The unicorn's flight was witnessed by a wise old soothsayer, who thought: "Galloping horse through the nighttime desert, white with one horn, you are a vision of surprise. Are you running from or to, I wonder?"

The beast drew close to the old man and stopped, stretching its neck to his side. "What do you search for with those eyes so wide?" thought the soothsayer, old and wise.

After a period of silence, the moon's light grew stronger, and her silver rays lit the sky. The soothsayer placed his hand on the unicorn's muzzle with compassion and a sigh. It must have been the full moon, with its power, you see, that made the soothsayer declare this prophecy.

"On this night your healing will begin. The pain and loneliness from your broken heart shall dissipate. Drink the water there," he said, pointing to a fresh spring filled with the moon's reflection. "As you quench your thirst, dear one, the water will wash away the stain of betrayal. You have found wisdom and purpose here in my oasis. Sleep now beside the mint and lavender. From this night forth, all who experience heartbreak may call upon you for divine aid, and into their dreams you shall gallop."

## SPELL TO HELP HEAL A BROKEN HEART

This spell calls on the prophecy of the soothsayer and the power of his oasis to relieve the pain of heartache and betrayal.

### *What you need:*
Either dried or fresh lavender, a sprig of fresh mint, spring water, one water glass, and a pen and paper.

**Instructions:**

Fill the water glass three-quarters full with spring water. Add a sprig of mint and let the glass sit under the light of a full moon for at least an hour (this is called "lunarizing" the water). Before you go to sleep, drink the water. Place the lavender under your pillow (if it's dried, you can use a sachet). Ask the unicorn to gallop into your dreams and heal your broken heart. Sleep with a pen and paper next to you to write down any messages you may receive while they are still fresh in your memory.

Why did I choose mint and lavender? Mint's magickal associations induce feelings of well-being and are known for offering protection. Heartbreak leaves one vulnerable and fatigued. Mint's spirits will help lift depression and create a healthy barrier in which to heal more readily.

Lavender's magickal associations increase clarity and feelings of peace. Often, heartbreak clouds your judgment and creates anxiety. In this spell, lavender is used to disperse anxiety, create clarity, and help induce dreams.

## ADDITIONAL RESOURCES

One important set of unicorn tapestries is found in the Cloisters Museum in New York, which is part of the Metropolitan Museum of Art. See *The Unicorn Tapestries* (1495–1505; acc. no. 37.80.6).

A second set of tapestries, equally important, is part of the collection of the Musée de Cluny, at the Musée national du Moyen Âge in Paris. See *The Lady and the Unicorn* (c. 1500), *http://musee-moyenage.fr*.

### Secondary sources

Cavallo, Adolfo Salvatore. *The Unicorn Tapestries at the Metropolitan Museum of Art* (New Haven, CT: Yale University Press, 1998).

Lavers, Chris. *The Natural History of Unicorns* (New York: HarperCollins, 2009).

Leo, Lawren. *Dragonflame: Tap into Your Reservoir of Power Using Talismans, Manifestation, and Visualization* (Pompton Plains, NJ: New Page Books, 2014).

## NOTES

1   I give instructions for dressing a candle in my book, *Dragonflame*, p. 126.

# Chapter 10

# THE GREAT MARE

The Roman Empire was vast at its apogee. Under the emperor Trajan, who reigned from 98 to 117 CE, it stretched from England to Syria, and from Germany to Egypt. Its estimated 70 million inhabitants had incredibly diverse religions and customs. Like the Egyptians, the Romans frequently adopted deities outside their pantheon. Although the army worshipped Mars and the Zoroastrian god Mithras, the cavalry (*alae*) was specifically responsible for spreading the cult of Epona, whose name is Gaulish for "divine mare."

## Epona

The cult of this Celtic horse goddess was most popular in the first three centuries CE. Horses had always played an important role in Celtic religion. According to the observations of the Roman historian Tacitus, the Celts kept pure white horses that had never been used for work in sacred groves.[1] The druids practiced hippomancy, the art of divination based on a horse's actions or appearance. For example, they interpreted neighs and snorts, or the sequence in which a horse moved its legs when it pulled a cart.

There are remote parallels between Epona and the older horse goddesses worshipped in Wales—Rhiannon, the Mare of Sovereignty—and in Ireland, where they worshipped Macha. But for the Celts, Epona played many roles. She was the goddess of fertility and death, and of both the Otherworld and the land of the living. She was a fierce warrior as well a loving mother. In the Roman period, she was almost always shown as a lovely young woman holding a cornucopia or *patera*, a shallow offering bowl, filled with grain, flanked by horses or mules. In other instances, she is shown riding side-saddle. There are representations of Epona in expensive mediums like marble and bronze, but also many in terra-cotta and wood. Temples dedicated to her are found in areas of Europe where the Roman soldiers were of Celtic blood, but there are a great number of extant altars that bear dedicatory inscriptions to her scattered throughout the empire. It is not surprising that they have been found in stables, where they were meant to protect the horses, especially when foaling.

Epona, in Roman times, was primarily the guardian of soldiers. The placement of grave markers, votive offerings, and inscribed statues near rivers, as well as depictions of her with a key, identify her as a psychopomp, a deity or spiritual being who accompanied and guided those who died to the Otherworld. Her feast day in ancient Rome was December 18, and the flower sacred to her is the rose. There is a humorous anecdote concerning worship of Epona in Roman writer Apuleius's novel, *The Golden Ass*. Here the protagonist, while in the form of an ass, eats roses that a devotee of the goddess had placed on her altar in a stable.[2]

# SPELL FOR BONDING WITH, PROTECTING, AND REMEMBERING ANIMAL COMPANIONS

Use this spell to bond with, protect, and remember animal companions through the power of the ancient Celtic horse goddess Epona.

### *What you need:*
Red, white, or yellow roses; dove's-blood ink; parchment paper; and a bowl of grain (oats will do just fine).

***Instructions:***

Follow the instructions found within the spell. Gather your roses and all else you'll need, then begin to read the spell slowly, as if Epona were speaking through you:

> *Bring me all your roses today—yellow, red, and white.*
>
> *With dove's-blood ink on parchment, this is what to write:*
>
> *Some pleasant words to honor me and then your heartfelt plea.*
>
> *Make an altar grand or plain, and put on top a bowl of grain.*
>
> *Place your petition on my altar under a rose deep red.*
>
> *State your pet's name thrice and forever you'll be wed.*
>
> *Another petition goes on my altar, but with a yellow rose aglow,*
>
> *Injury, attack, and harm, your pet will never know.*
>
> *A last petition goes on my altar under a rose forever white.*
>
> *Your pet has passed, but lives with me where there is never night.*

> *Great Goddess Epona! Punish those who would harm our animal companions;*
>
> *Bless those who keep them safe and offer them loving homes.*
>
> *May my roses and petitions honor you and keep you at my side in peace and war.*

Why did I choose red, yellow, and white roses? Red roses are associated with love—the deepest bond. Yellow roses are associated with friendship and as an offering to Epona for protection. White roses are associated with resurrection and renewal.

Why did I choose dove's-blood ink, parchment paper, and oats? Dove's-blood ink is used to seal this spell's promise and to show loyalty. Parchment paper (or any stiff paper) is traditionally used in magickal operations to remind practitioners that this is not a mundane act. Oats are simple to find at the market and are magickally associated with health and abundance.

## ADDITIONAL RESOURCES

For a thorough, well-documented, and helpful site on Epona, see: *http://epona.net* (accessed 5/20/2018).

### Primary sources

Apuleius. *The Golden Ass*, trans. Sarah Ruden (New Haven, CT: Yale University Press, 2011).

Tacitus, Cornelius. *Tacitus I, Agricola. Germania. Dialogus*, trans. M. Hutton and W. Peterson, rev. ed. (Cambridge, MA: Harvard University Press, 1914).

### Secondary sources

Bullia, Cassandra. *Transcending Borders: An Analysis of Epona Worship Cross-Culturally and Her Roman Adoption.* Retrieved from *https://academia.edu* (accessed 6/6/2018).

Davidson, Hilda R. E. *Myths and Symbols in Pagan Europe: Early Scandinavian and Celtic Religions* (Manchester, England: Manchester University Press, 1988).

Hughes, Kristoffer. *From the Cauldron Born: Exploring the Magic of Welsh Legend and Lore* (Woodbury, MN: Llewellyn, 2017).

Linduff, Katheryn. "Epona: A Celt among the Romans," *Latoma* 38, 4 (1979), pp. 817–837.

Waddell, John. "Equine Cults and Celtic Goddesses," *Emania Bulletin of the Navan Research Group* 24 (2018), pp. 5–18.

Winkle, Jeffrey T. "Epona Salvatrix? Isis and the Horse Goddess in Apuleius' Metamorphoses," *Ancient Narrative* 12 (2015).

## NOTES

1  Tacitus, *Germania*, IX–X.
2  Apuleius, 3.7.

# Chapter 11

# THE PAGAN HORSE

The horse played a central role in Viking and Teutonic (Germanic) religious ceremonies and magick. For instance, there is a ritual for cursing in *seidhr*, a form of Norse magick, in which a horse's head is mounted on a rune-inscribed "shaming pole" (*nidstang*). It was hoisted aloft or planted in the ground and made to face the enemy. Horse burial, however, was the most common use of equine magick in Viking, as well as Celtic and Anglo-Saxon, practices. This attests to the noble position the horse held in these societies, for they placed nearly no other animal in their tombs.

## Viking Horse Magick

Horse sacrifice was customary for burials as well as for securing the fertility of the land. Examples of this extend from the British Isles to Scythia (present-day Iran). In graves, horses not only marked social status, but also provided a means of transportation to and within the spirit world. They may also have been symbolic of the sun. Archaeologists have excavated and studied thousands of horse burials. A 10th-century chronicler, Ahmad ibn Fadlan, gives an eyewitness account of a burial he saw during his travels as part of the embassy of the Abbasid Caliph of Baghdad. He writes of a large ship burial among the Rus (Volga Vikings) in his *Risala* ("journal") of c. 921–22 CE. The elaborate ceremony took many days and, at one point, included the use of an intoxicated

young slave girl who was made to have sex with multiple partners, after which she was killed and buried with the dead man.
At another stage in this same event, two horses were made to
run until they were overheated and were then dismembered and
added to the grave.

Horse sacrifices were an integral part of solemnizing ceremonies, such as the one that was held every nine years for the
Swedish provinces. Adam of Bremen records that nine humans,
horses, and dogs were sacrificed to placate the gods, their bodies
hung from trees in sacred groves near the great temple at Uppsala.
As a result, these trees became divine entities.[1] The tales in the
Icelandic writer Snorri Sturluson's 13th-century *Prose Edda* are
also filled with references to the ritualistic use of horses, including an instance in which a horse was cut apart and cooked in a
broth in which the king was meant to bathe and to drink. The
horse, it must be remembered, served as food in many societies.

Sturluson also names the mighty steeds that served the Nordic
deities, as well as the horses that created the cycles of night
and day and the seasons—Hrímfaxi (Frost Mane) and Skinfaxi
(Shining Mane). Sturluson was penning myths passed down orally
for generations, as the images on the earlier 8th-to-11th-centu-
ry-CE memorial runes and picture stones from Gotland Island,
Sweden, make clear.

Perhaps the best known of the Viking steeds is the god Odin's
eight-legged stallion named Sleipnir (Sliding One), which carried
him through the air. Odin's wife, Frigg, the goddess of marriage,
love, and precognition, had a divine messenger named Gná,
whose mount, Hófvarpnir (Hoof-Thrower), could fly through
the physical and spiritual realms and travel on water. It is here
that we will choose to focus, on the more lighthearted nature of
Vikings, as we turn to Frigg for help with love.

# SPELL FOR A SUCCESSFUL LOVE LIFE

This spell calls on the powers of the Norse goddess Frigg, her divine messenger, Gná, and Gná's magickal mount, Hófvarpnir (Hoof-Thrower), to dispel loneliness and to bring you success in your love life.

**What you need:**

Florida water (a sweet, citrusy cologne water used traditionally in Hoodoo, Voodoo, Santería, and Wicca for a variety of ritual work), a Pyrex bowl, parchment paper, one pen with black ink, one pen with red ink, and a long-nosed lighter.

**Instructions:**

On a piece of parchment paper, using a pen with black ink, write "Frigg," "Gná," and "Hófvarpnir" in large letters, layered over one another. First, write "Frigg." Then, on top of that, write "Gná." On top of "Gná," write "Hófvarpnir." Center these layered names on the front side of the parchment. On the other side of the parchment, using the pen with black ink, write out this spell:

*I hold my hand out into the ether,*

*For I do not wish to be alone in this lifetime.*

*Frigg, goddess of love and marriage, surely there is another holding [his/her] hand out as well.*

*Reweave part of destiny's web for me;*

*Bring us together; find me that treasure that seems to be hidden so well—true love.*

*Send your messenger and her beautiful horse; let them race over the waters of the ethers.*

*A successful love life is the future I have always wanted to create.*

*Catch it in a flash; hold it in an orb.*

*Let it be now.*

Each day for four days (that means you'll be writing five days in total), trace the spell that you have written in black ink using the pen with red ink. On the fifth day, put the parchment paper in the Pyrex bowl and pour Florida water over it until it is soaked completely. Light it with a long-nosed lighter. (For safety reasons, please use caution when working with fire!) Blow the ashes to the wind and make your wish in affirmation form:

*Now I have a successful love life!*

Why did I choose Florida water? Primarily for its flammable property (it has a high alcohol content), but also for its pleasing scent of clove, orange, and lavender, which is appropriate for attracting the spirits of love.

Why did I choose five days for the spell? Five is the magickal number of the pentagram. Each point of the pentagram represents an element: air, water, fire, earth, and spirit. Together, these five elements create life. Blowing the ashes into the wind is symbolic of blowing them into the ether, where your spell takes on a life of its own.

# Svetovid

According to the Danish historian Saxo Grammaticus (1150–1220), Rügen Island, off the northern coast of present-day Germany, was the focal point for the worship of Svetovid (Svantovit), the Slavic god of war, abundance, and fertility. The island made a distinct impression on Saxo and he felt it worthy to have both its monuments and its customs described for posterity's sake. He tells of a gigantic red wooden temple hung with rich purple textiles that held the cult statue of Svetovid. The statue was immense beyond imagining, with four heads and four necks, two facing front and two back, each looking in a different direction.

What Saxo found most curious, however, was the god's prized possession—an oracular white stallion. The Slavs, he recounts, held this horse in such high esteem that it was a sacrilege to pluck even a single hair from its mane or tail. The sacred horse was cared for by a long-bearded priest, who used it for soothsaying. The people believed that Svetovid rode the stallion to war nightly against all those who did not worship him. As evidence, they cited the fact that, according to all accounts, the horse was clean when it was retired to the stables at night, but every morning was found spattered with dried mud, sweat, and blood.

Before going to war, Svetovid's followers consulted the priest to seek signs of the god's consent through hippomancy (horse divination). After praying, the priest led the horse through three equidistant rows of crossed spears laid out on the ground. If its right front foot did not lead in three successive paces, it was taken to be a bad omen and all plans for battle were canceled.

## SPELL TO STOP BULLIES

Where there is deep hatred, tunnel vision, bigotry, and discrimination, a countermeasure is necessary. Enter the Slavic god of war, Svetovid, and his oracular stallion. This pure-white, sacred stallion is a wise, fearless, all-seeing force that is ready and able to do battle for you.

***What you need:***
Pen, paper, lighter or matches, and a Pyrex bowl or large cauldron.

***Instructions:***
At midnight (for the horse rode out to battle only at night), write the name(s) of the person, persons, or group that is bullying you on a piece of paper. Using your right hand only, draw an "X" over the name(s) three times, one atop the other. This is symbolic of the white stallion's sign that you will be victorious in battle—it had

to step over three sets of crossed spears, leading each time with its right hoof. Now, since the god Svetovid rode the stallion, seal the bully's fate by writing his or her name over it all in large letters. Crumple the paper in your right hand by making a fist. Place it in the Pyrex bowl or cauldron and light it. Burn it until only ashes remain (no paper left to litter). Now, imagine your enemies scattered and vanquished as you blow the ashes to the wind.

## ADDITIONAL RESOURCES

### *Primary sources*

Byock, Jesse, trans. *The Prose Edda* (London: Penguin Classics, 2005).

Herodotus. *The Histories*, ed. Paul Cartledge, trans. Tom Holland (New York: Penguin Books, 2015). See Book IV for a lively account of horse burial in royal tombs.

Saxo Grammaticus. *The First Nine Books of the Danish History of Saxo Grammaticus*, trans. Oliver Elton with notes by Frederick York Powell (London: David Nutt, 1894).

Smyser, H. M. "Ibn Fadlan's Account of the Rus with Some Commentary and Some Allusions to *Beowulf.*" In Jess B. Bessinger, Jr. and Robert P. Creed, ed., *Franciplegius: Medieval and Linguistic Studies in Honor of Francis Peabody Magoun, Jr.* (New York: New York University Press, 1965), pp. 92–119.

### *Secondary sources*

Duczko, Wladyslaw. *Viking Rus: Studies on the Presence of Scandinavians in Eastern Europe* (Leiden, Netherlands: Brill, 2004). On the account of the Rus funeral in Ibn Fadlan's *Risala*, see pp. 137–154.

Hermes, Nizar F. "Utter Alterity or Pure Humanity: Barbarian Turks, Bulghars, and Rus (Vikings) in the Remarkable *Risala* of Ibn Fadlan." In *The [European] Other in Medieval Arabic Literature and Culture: Ninth-Twelfth Century AD* (New York: Palgrave Macmillan, 2012), pp. 80–84.

Ivantchik, Askold. "The Funeral of Scythian Kings: The Historical Reality and the Description of Herodotus (IV, 71–72)." In L. Bonfante, ed., *European Barbarians* (Cambridge, England: Cambridge University Press, 2011), pp. 71–106.

Lomand, Ulla. "The Horse and Its Role in Icelandic Burial Practices, Mythology, and Society." In Anders Andren, Kristina Jennbert, and Catharina Raudvere, ed., *Old Norse Religion in Long-term Perspectives: Origins, Changes, and Interactions* (Lund, Sweden: Nordic Academic, 2006), pp. 130–133.

Lunde, Paul, and Caroline Stone. *Ibn Fadlan and the Land of Darkness: Arab Travellers in the Far North* (London: Penguin Classics, 2011).

Mitchell, Stephen A. *Witchcraft and Magic in the Norse Middle Ages* (Philadelphia: University of Pennsylvania Press, 2010).

Page, R. I. *Chronicles of the Vikings: Records, Memorials, and Myths* (Toronto: University of Toronto Press, 1995).

Rowsell, Thomas. "Riding to the Afterlife: The Role of Horses in Early Medieval North-Western Europe," MA Thesis, University College of London, 2012.

Shenk, Peter. *To Valhalla by Horseback? Horse Burial in Scandinavia during the Viking Age* (Oslo, Norway: The Center for Viking and Medieval Studies, University of Oslo, 2002).

**NOTES**

1 Page, 1995, p. 221.

# Chapter 12

# THE SAINT'S HORSE

How could some of the most famous military saints have performed their miraculous deeds without equally miraculous mounts? It is sad, however, that Christian hagiographers (authors of the lives of saints) of the Middle Ages and earlier, unlike the Greek mythographers, did not record these horses' names. Nonetheless, the stories of these mounts have come down to us in the tales of their famous riders.

## St. George, the Dragon Slayer

Multiple versions of the tale of St. George the dragon slayer have come down to us—rooted, perhaps, in myths like Bellerophon on Pegasus defeating the Chimera. This saint is reputed to have served as a member of the cavalry in the Roman army during the reign of emperors Diocletian (b. 244 CE, r. 284–305, d. 314 CE) and Maximian (b. 250 CE, r. 286–305), by whom he was martyred. He hailed from Cappadocia, a region in present-day Turkey. It is said that he rode a fearless, brilliant-white stallion into combat against a dragon that was claiming the lives of the townspeople by poisoning a water supply and then demanding youths and maidens as daily tribute sacrifices.

The moment St. George spears the dragon, thereby saving the local king's daughter, is the scene on countless Byzantine icons and in many Renaissance paintings. He is one of the most popular Christian saints, and his defeat of the dragon embodies the theme of the triumph of good over evil. He is the patron saint of England, Portugal, Lithuania, and Greece, and his feast day is April 23.

# St. Eligius and St. Dunstan

St. Eligius (588–660) is the patron saint of horses, veterinarians, farriers, and metalworkers of all types. His feast day is December 1. He is most often shown as a bishop, wearing a pointed hat, or mitre, and carrying the crook proper to his office. But he is also shown holding an anvil or horseshoe. According to one anecdote, he shod a problematic horse by amputating the animal's leg, attaching the shoe, and then miraculously restoring the leg. But the traditional folklore of horseshoes bringing luck probably comes from a later period in Anglo-Saxon England and the encounter between a monk, St. Dunstan, and the devil.

St. Dunstan (c. 909–988), onetime archbishop of Canterbury, was multitalented. His feast day is May 19 and he is regularly depicted with a blacksmith's tongs. His 11th-century biographer, Osbern of Canterbury, relates that, in addition to his intellectual prowess, Dunstan was a harpist, a silversmith (he is the patron saint of those who work in this field), and a calligrapher and illuminator of manuscripts. In one variant of the saint-devil interaction, Dunstan was playing the harp when the devil attempted to disturb the heavenly music by making loud noises. Dunstan put down his instrument and reached for the hot tongs with which he worked metal. He clamped them down on the devil's nose. Pain rendered the devil defenseless, and Dunstan shod one of his hooves. The devil howled until Dunstan removed the horseshoe, but not before the saint had him promise to avoid all abodes where a horseshoe was hung over the door and to leave those who lived there in peace.

In addition to the Christian tales explaining the potency of a horseshoe as an apotropaic or good-luck charm, legend has it that iron is repulsive to malicious magickal creatures. Using seven nails to hang a horseshoe was believed to increase its power. The position for hanging a horseshoe is disputed: ends up, for some, creates a vessel to hold all good luck; for others, ends down showers luck on all those who enter. It is not uncommon to see horseshoes hung in both positions, one above the other, especially in barns or on ship masts.

## SPELL FOR A HORSESHOE BLESSING

This spell uses the magickal power of the horsehoe to bring blessings and good luck to those who perform it. It also banishes the evil eye. In this particular practice, the horseshoe is hung with the points up.

*What you need:*
A horseshoe, a hammer, and nails (to hang the horseshoe above your doorway); agrimony (powdered agrimony is easiest to use); quick-light charcoal; a lighter; a small ceramic or Pyrex bowl; and enough sand to fill the bowl.

*Instructions:*
Hang the horseshoe with the ends pointing up (like the crescent moon) above the front doorway either inside or outside the house you want to bless. Fill the small bowl with sand. Light the quick-light charcoal with the lighter and place it on top of the sand in the bowl. Sprinkle a pinch of agrimony onto the charcoal. Chant this blessing three times as the smoke from the agrimony rises onto the horseshoe:

> *Horseshoe hanging above my door,*
>
> *Ends up to keep good luck secure,*
>
> *I consecrate you with all my heart.*
>
> *And now with true intent I start.*
>
> *Agrimony work for me;*

*Remove these from my destiny:*

*All evil, evil eyes, curses, negativity, upset conditions, and black magick!*

*I thank you now, god and goddess, Dunstan too.*

*With horse and iron the devil got his due;*

*Peace and wealth may stay with me.*

*And as my will so mote it be!*

Why did I choose agrimony for this spell? The magickal properties of agrimony are well known for dispersing negativity and creating a shield of protection. You can also drink agrimony tea prior to starting this blessing to add more power.

# St. Joan of Arc

The horse is also a key iconographic element (visual attribute) in images and statues of another equestrian soldier. This soldier is, however, the most unlikely member of the male-dominated, hetero-normative cavalry in the Middle Ages—the diminutive St. Joan of Arc (c. 1412–1431). When a "voice" told young Joan to go to a prominent captain to obtain men-at-arms, she replied: "I'm just a poor maid who can neither ride nor fight."[1] The "voice," and her legacy, have proven her wrong on both accounts. The so-called Maid of Orléans, whose early childhood was spent learning to sew and work on a farm, rode like a professional when she left her peasant surroundings. She cut her hair, donned men's clothing, took up arms, and traversed the countryside to meet the French aristocracy and lead them in battle to defeat the English. Against overwhelming odds, she played a key role in having Charles VII (b. 1403, r. 1422–1461) formally crowned king in 1429.

Aside from her equestrian skills, we know that Joan had supernatural gifts. As a clairaudient and visionary, she received directives from heavenly voices and heard the pealing of church bells.

She saw brilliant otherworldly lights, and she conversed with St. Catherine and St. Margaret, as well as with the archangels Michael and Gabriel. The most eloquent testimony to Joan's calling as a soldier-knight is found in a poem written nearly half a century after she was burned at the stake. Her bond to her horse is the subject of Linda McCarriston's *La Coursier de Jeanne d'Arc* (*The Charger of Joan of Arc*).[2]

McCarriston doubles the cruelty of the saint's martyrdom by recounting that, before the flames consumed her, Joan was made to watch while her gray-and-white dappled Percheron was burned to death. Joan's rapport with her horse was incredibly important to a contemporary understanding of her sexuality. Women certainly rode ponies and hunted on spirited horses, but it was outside the norm of femininity at the time to wear men's clothing and armor or to ride a charger or warhorse. (*Coursier* or *destrier* are the words in Old French; Joan specifically said she was riding *un demi-coursier*.) For historian Marina Warner, Joan's androgyny upset the "natural order" and made her more angelic than human.[3] More recently, however, Gabrielle Bychowski emphasizes that Joan "may have identified as trans,"[4] given that the English government accused her of being a witch and a heretic because she wore men's clothing. In the end, we can be sure of three things: Joan's purity of resolve, her faith, and her love for France. She herself said it quite simply: "I am sent from God."[5] Joan is one of the nine minor patron saints of France and her feast day is May 30.

# SPELL FOR CLAIRAUDIENCE AND GUIDANCE

This spell calls on horse magick to let you share in Joan of Arc's power of clairaudience and wisdom. Use it to seek guidance in any situation, especially one in which you feel lost. It is also helpful for anyone trying to determine how they identify sexually.

**What you need:**

Horsetail herb, quick-light charcoal tablets, a censer or other "fire-proof" container, and a lighter.

**Instructions:**

Light a piece of quick-light charcoal and arrange it safely in your censer. Now, prepare yourself magickally by imagining a circle of fire around you. Say to yourself:

> *No person, spirit, entity, energy, or thought form can cross this*
> *circle except those who have my best intentions at heart.*

Calm and center yourself. Sprinkle a pinch or two of horsetail herb onto the burning quick-light charcoal in your censer. Fan the smoke from the burning herb toward you as you say this spell three times three:

> *Future so hard to come by,*
>
> *Wisdom on which to rely,*
>
> *Open up and, out of the sky,*
>
> *Let fall words that tell no lie;*
>
> *Secret tongue I finally descry,*
>
> *Perfect path—bullseye!*

Why did I choose horsetail herb? Horsetail herb is associated with the planet Saturn, which governs time, the mind's eye, wisdom, and psychic ability. Horsetail herb has the power to locate hard-to-find answers and to reveal hidden secrets.

### ADDITIONAL RESOURCES

Jeffrey Burton Russell (1972), p. 76, cites a Carolingian Capitulary (erroneously known as the *Canon Episcopi*), stating that "wicked women" participated in midnight rides on various beasts, including horses, under the influence of Diana. This would become commonplace in aligning women and horses throughout the Middle Ages and beyond in witch hunts. For more on this phenomenon, see Claude Lecouteux, *Phantom Armies of the Night: The Wild Hunt and the Ghostly Processions of the Undead*, trans. Jon E. Graham (Rochester, VT: Inner Traditions, 2011).

**Primary sources**

Jacobus de Voragine. *The Golden Legend: Readings on the Saints*, trans. William Granger Ryan, vol. 1 (Princeton, NJ: Princeton University Press, 1993), pp. 238–242.

Winterbottom, Michael, and Michael Lapidge, ed. and trans. *The Early Lives of St. Dunstan* (Oxford, England: Oxford University Press, 2012).

**Secondary sources**

Barrett, W. P. trans. *The Trial of Jeanne d'Arc* (New York: Gotham House, Inc., 1932). Retrieved from *https://sourcebooks.fordham.edu* (accessed 11/2/2018).

Bychowski, Gabrielle. "Gender, Sexism, and the Middle Ages, Part 3: Were There Transgender People in the Middle Ages?" *The PublicMedievalist.Com* (November 2018). Retrieved from *https://publicmedievalist.com* (accessed 11/2/2018).

Gauvard, Claude, Alain de Libera, Michel Zink, dirs. *Dictionnaire du Moyen Âge* (Paris: Quadrige/Presses Universitaires de France, 2002).

Hyland, Ann. *The Horse in the Middle Ages* (Thrupp, England: Sutton Publishing, 1999).

Illes, Judika. *Encyclopedia of Mystics, Saints & Sages: A Guide to Asking for Protection, Wealth, Happiness, and Everything Else!* (New York: HarperOne, 2011).

Kaiser, Anton. *Joan of Arc: A Study in Charismatic Women's Leadership* (Rapid City, SD: Black Hills Books, 2017).

McCarriston, Linda. "La Coursier de Jeanne d'Arc." In *Little River: New and Selected Poems* (Knockeven, Ireland: Salmon Poetry, 1993); available in full online at: *https://poets.org* (accessed 12/15/2018).

Meltzer, Françoise. *For Fear of the Fire: Joan of Arc and the Limits of Subjectivity* (Chicago: Chicago University Press, 2001).

Ramsay, Nigel. *St. Dunstan: His Life, Times, and Cult* (Rochester, NY: Boydell Press, 1992).

Russell, Jeffrey Burton. *Witchcraft in the Middle Ages* (Ithaca, NY: Cornell University Press, 1972).

Seward, Desmond. *The Hundred Years War: The English in France 1337–1453* (New York and London: Penguin Books, 1999).

Warner, Marina. *Joan of Arc: The Image of Female Heroism* (Oxford, England: Oxford University Press, 1981).

### NOTES

1  Barrett, 1932, XII, 160.
2  The poem is available in full online at *https://poets.org.*
3  Warner, 1981, p. 146.
4  Bychowski, 2018.
5  Barrett, 1932, p. 81.

*Chapter 13*

# THE JADE HORSE

In China, jade possessed a function that superseded its decorative value. In the 4,300-year-old city in the Loess Highland now called Shimao (its original name is unknown), the builders ritualistically placed jade artifacts between the blocks of all the city's structures. Together with skulls from human sacrifices buried in key spots, the jade was probably thought to give Shimao enduring power and spiritual protection.

Although there is evidence that there was a proper civilization in China as early as 9000 BCE, the domesticated horse was probably introduced there around 3000 BCE. We can ascribe the invention of the stirrup (around 322 CE), the horse collar, and a harnessing system based on the breast strap to the Chinese. Horses were held in such high esteem in China and were so important that both they and the chariots and carriages they drew are regularly found in tombs along with their owners as early as the Shang dynasty (around 1600–1100 BCE).

In Chinese religion and mythology, the horse was combined with the dragon and thought to have the mystical gift of flight. The Tienma (Celestial or Heavenly Horse), a combination of myth and reality, was most likely the ancestor of today's long-legged, silvery-coated Akhal Teke, a breed that originated in modern Turkmenistan. The Han emperor Wudi, who ruled from 140 to 87 BCE, began a war to acquire these horses for his cavalry, and various poets deemed them "waterborn," just like dragons.[1] An understanding of the Chinese veneration of both the horse and jade are important in order to understand the way in which you can apply them to broaden your spirituality and strengthen your magick. That veneration can be seen clearly in this Chinese folktale, in which both the subject and the medium bestow meaning and power on a small statuette.

## Tienma (Tian Ma), the Celestial Horse

Richly embroidered silk robes hissed, and precariously high headdresses sighed in the building wind as the sun began to set over the funeral celebration. Dense incense smoke floated out of bronze censers; rows of impeccably dressed soldiers and aristocrats stood to attention; and groups of horses fidgeted nervously, their gilded bronze trappings jingling and gleaming. Finally, the shaman spoke. Pointing his bony finger, he intoned: "My Lord of Khotan, the omens are most auspicious. Observe! The sky is parded over with white clouds like the coat of the snow leopard and dappled like the celestial horse! Take heed! They begin to flame like the scales of a fiery dragon as the sun ends its course and sets in the west. Surely your child has passed over peacefully into the celestial realms." No tears were discernible on the ruler's wizened face, but a mother's sob emerged from deep inside the enclosed chariot.

The Lord of Khotan said: "Have the court artist make a likeness from the finest white mutton-fat jade that shows my child dressed as a warrior riding the winged celestial horse and place it in his tomb. Thus, he can rightly join his ancestors in the realm of the immortals."

And so, it was done. To this day, the precious statuette resides in the Shanxi Xianyang Municipal Museum, depicting a warrior grasping the mane of a horse flying over clouds.

# SPELL TO WED YOURSELF TO GOOD LUCK

The old adage, "Something old, something new, something borrowed, and something blue" plays a role in this spell to bring good fortune. In it, an old plate or bowl covers the first item—something old; a borrowed plate or bowl covers the third item—something borrowed; jade is something new; and periwinkle (also known as Sorcerer's Violet) is something blue. The spell draws on the special powers of jade to bring good fortune.

***What you need:***

At least four ounces of periwinkle[2] (the blue flower, not the leaf); a piece of jade that you can wear or carry (tumbled, necklace, bracelet, ring, etc.), preferably in the shape of a horse; a borrowed small plate or bowl and an old plate or bowl large enough to hold your piece of jade. You'll also need a small amount of timothy hay.

***Instructions:***

Place the "borrowed" small plate or bowl to the left of your jade and the "old" plate or bowl to the right. Fill the "borrowed" small plate or bowl with the timothy hay as an offering to the spirit that presides over your piece of jade. Now, with reverance, place your piece of jade on or in the "old" plate or bowl to its right. Cover it as much as possible, using all the periwinkle. Begin to slow your breathing as you calm and center yourself. Hold your hands over the periwinkle and jade. Imagine light-blue flames the color of the periwinkle pouring forth from your palms and into the jade. Say:

> *Spirit of the Sorcerer's Violet, cleanse the stone that finds itself under your leaves, then bind it to me—my soul to its soul, its soul to mine. So mote it be.*

While still holding your hands over the jade and while still feeling the blue, fiery energy emanating from your palms, chant this
spell as many times as you like, but not fewer than three:

*Hurtle over your obstacles,*

*Jump over the stick of the broom;*

*Smash the glass and say I do.*

*Something is old;*

*Something is new;*

*Something must be borrowed;*

*Find something blue.*

*Work your magick;*

*Cast the spell.*

*Forever, good luck,*

*I'm wed to you.*

Leave the jade under the periwinkle for twenty-four hours. Then
remove the jade from the flowers. Throw the periwinkle back to
Mother Earth and say:

*Thank you, kind spirits. You are released.*

Do the same with the timothy hay.

The jade is now ready to be placed in an area that holds significance for you, or, if it's tumbled, to be carried on your person
(pocket, purse, brazier, etc.). If it is a piece of jewelry, it is ready
to be worn. Please read the rules below, however. They are an
important part of this spell and you must follow them for it to
work properly.

### Some rules:

- The jade will prove to be more potent if it is in the shape
  of a horse, but will still work nicely if it is tumbled or
  shaped otherwise.

- If the jade is in the shape of a horse, you do not need to carry or wear it. Instead, you can place it somewhere special or in an area of your home, office, or workspace that holds importance in some significant emotional or magickal manner.

- You do not need to carry or wear the jade every day, as long as you pay attention to it at least two or three times a week—cleanse it magickally, rub some good luck oil on it, dust it, talk to it, etc. I like to clean mine with a mixture of essential oil of mugwort and water on the new moon, full moon, or both. Most of the time, I just pat it on the head and say: "Bring me good luck."

- The jade should only be worn, carried, or placed by itself. The jade is married to you. It will be jealous if you carry it in a mixture of other stones or if you wear it with other jewelry adorned with stones. It will be very jealous if you place it in an inconspicuous place or next to another precious or semiprecious stone.

- If your jade breaks or is lost, you must repeat this spell using a new piece of jade. But there's a caveat: the jade must be given to you by someone else. You may not purchase another piece for this spell the second time around, or the third, fourth, or fifth for that matter. Your first piece of jade broke or was lost because it was finished serving its purpose. When it is time for you to repeat this spell, another piece will present itself. Once it does, then you may purchase another piece in the shape of a horse if you like, or use the piece that somebody gave to you.

- When using this spell, only enchant one piece of jade at a time.

Why did I choose periwinkle? Periwinkle is used to enhance the sex life, and for marital bliss, fidelity, and protection.

For an interesting study of the metaphysical and geological properties of jade, see: Nicholas Pearson, *The Seven Archetypal Stones: Their Spiritual Powers and Teachings* (Rochester, VT: Inner Traditions, 2016), pp. 38–81.

For the background on the Akhal-Teke, see "History of the Akhal-Teke" on the official website of the International Association of Akhal-Teke Breeding (MAAK), *http://maakcenter.org* (accessed 12/26/2018).

### Secondary sources

Cooke, Bill, "The Horse in Chinese History." In Cooke (2000), pp. 27–62.

——————, dir. *Imperial China: The Art of the Horse in Chinese History*, exh. cat. (Lexington, KY: Kentucky Horse Park; in conjunction with Prospect, KY: Harmony House Publishers, 2000); cat. no. 120, p. 137, "Winged Horse and Rider," Jade, Western Han Dynasty (206 BCE–8 CE), Shanxi Xianyang Municipal Museum. With thanks for the reference to Stacy Pearson at the School of Oriental and Asian Studies, University College, London.

Jaang, L., Z. Sun, J. Shao, and M. Li. "When Peripheries Were Centres: A Preliminary Study of the Shimao-centred Polity in the Loess Highland, China," *Antiquity* 92 (364) (2018), pp. 1008–1022. Retrieved from doi:10.15184/aqy.2018.31 (accessed 11/29/2018).

Jarus, Owen. "Massive Pyramid, Lost City and Ancient Human Sacrifices Unearthed in China," *Live Science* (August 23, 2018). Retrieved from *https://livescience.com*, with thanks to David Nishimura.

Ni, Xueting Christine. *From Kuan Yin to Chairman Mao: The Essential Guide to Chinese Deities* (Newburyport, MA: Weiser Books, 2018). For the story of the horse-headed goddess,

Lei Zu, see pp. 148–151; on Ma Shen, horse deities, see pp. 217–219.

## NOTES

1  Cooke, "The Horse," pp. 41–44; Ni, 2018, p. 218, writes that the mythical dragon-horse, ancestor of all horses, is Long Ma.
2  Please be sure to increase the amount of periwinkle to suit the size of your piece of jade. You need enough to cover it.

*Chapter 14*

# THE LUNAR HORSE

Beware reader! Not all religious tales are pleasant, and some-times the path to esoteric enlightenment is sullied with offal. The choice is yours; turn back now or just step around anything you may find offensive until the path is once again clear. Is this not, after all, the case in life itself? It is certainly the case in the ancient Japanese myth of the sun goddess, Amaterasu, which is drawn from the sacred text of the Shinto religion, *The Kojiki* (*An Account of Ancient Matters*). This myth has repulsive elements, but ultimately it edifies.

## Amaterasu and Susanowo

The tale starts with the first parent, Izanagi, giving missions to the three noble children— Amaterasu, goddess of the sun; Tsukiyomi, god of the moon; and Susanowo, who, though meant to rule the world, instead became ruler of the realm of the dead through his base actions. In a fit of rage, Susanowo spread excrement through-out Amaterasu's rice fields and then secretly defecated under her throne in the palace where she was about to participate in the sacred rite of tasting the first rice from the harvest. His actions made her ill and defiled the rite.

To add to the insult, he broke a tile in the roof of the sacred weaving hall and hurled the skin of a heavenly piebald (spotted or dappled) pony he had flayed at her. This wounded her, causing her weaving loom to stab her in her genitals. Amaterasu, sickly, hurt, and offended by her brother's actions, fled to the perpetual darkness of the heavenly rock cave. Only the sound of the gods' uproarious laughter at the obscene dance of the goddess Ame-no-Uzume managed to lure her out again so she could take her place as the all-illuminating sun.

The odd story of Susanowo's use of the pony's skin very likely has deep magickal meaning. Normally, an animal is flayed from tail to head (*utsuhagi*), in accordance with its anatomy. But Susanowo used the reverse method (*sakahagi*), which is both laborious and counterproductive. In ancient Japanese magickal practices, reciting spells while performing reverse actions like drinking rice wine and clapping turned actions that were otherwise benedictions for health and a long life into curses. Obviously, these actions must take place on an astral level, because it is impossible in the physical realm to drink or clap backward. So, the flaying was meant to cause Amaterasu's death, as is apparent in both the wound to her genitals—the source of life—and her flight to the rock cave. In ancient Japan, aristocrats buried their dead in rock chambers, and the word *iwagakuru,* which means "concealment in rocks," was a euphemism for "death." It is even arguable that the horse's dappling marked it as a moon animal, turning Susanowo's action into an ill omen, since, by flaying the horse, he was trying to destroy light.[1] It is only fitting that we turn to Amaterasu's brilliant beauty to add balance to such an ugly tale. Amaterasu, as goddess of the sun, can assist you in all matters, but is especially inclined to gift you with inner and outer beauty. Over years of meditation and working with her energy, she revealed a portion of her mysteries to me in a simple, but profound, manner by speaking to me clairaudiently: "In the Western tradition, you speak of the Man in the Moon, because the Mare on the Moon could be construed as the features of an old man, even though you revere it as a female deity. So I, Amaterasu, am the Woman in the Sun, even though you are accustomed to know the sun as a masculine deity."

I thought long and hard on these words, realizing that I could not impose my cultural upbringing and traditions on a spell dedicated to a goddess worshipped halfway around the world. And then I understood Amaterasu's statement and how I could apply it to my own appreciation of and reverence for her.

As the Man in the Moon represents the masculine strength of a distinctly feminine orb at its fullest, so does the Woman in the Sun represent the feminine touch and taming of the blazing and distinctly masculine orb at the center of our solar system. I also believe that she revealed herself as the Woman in the Sun—an avant-garde, unapologetic goddess—to break stereotypes and help us better understand the universe and its magick in general. That insight is central to understanding this next spell.

## SPELL FOR BEAUTY AND PHYSICAL ATTRACTION

As I meditated on Amaterasu for this spell, I intuitively decided to burn frankincense and myrrh. As it turns out, this combination of fragrance was the key to understanding her mysteries.

For Westerners, these two essences are most familiar for their documented use in the mummification process in ancient Egypt and as two of the three gifts the Wise Men gave to the Christ child in the Bible. Amaterasu chose these resins as a cultural bridge for spellwork, whereas pine or sandalwood would have been the more traditional Shinto fragrances.

In order to bring focus into this spell (or any spell or rite), myrrh is quite helpful. Whether the resin is burned on charcoal or the essential oil is used to bless a candle or to make a tea, its properties help practitioners focus on the true intent and inner workings of the spell. Myrrh is associated with the sun and can induce peace and contentment, thereby joining us to Amaterasu's gentle magickal current.

Frankincense, on the other hand, is used in the Western tradition to invoke solar deities and the active, aggressive energies of the astral realm and universe. Myrrh and frankincense harmonize when you use them together. They become the yin and yang of the magickal world, a model in miniature of Amaterasu's power. As the sun is projective, and what is traditionally considered masculine, her female energy found within it seems to create a dichotomy that is resolved only when we understand that her energy is a consistent and gentle glow, a motherly nourishment flowing from a life-giving star that illuminates the Self.

The use of frankincense and myrrh in this spell manifests the energies of life, balance, harmony, illumination, and radiance, laying waste to inner discord and ugliness. They are in accord with the prime energies of Amaterasu: inner beauty, outer beauty, harmony, and love.

### What you need:
One tumbled citrine (natural citrine or heat-treated amethyst will both serve your purpose), essential oil of frankincense, and essential oil of myrrh.

### Instructions:
After drawing a bath for yourself, add three drops of frankincense and three drops of myrrh directly into the bathwater. Put the tumbled citrine in the bath as well. Take your time getting into the bath. Once you are relaxed (you may want to fold a towel to put behind your head), center yourself by focusing on your mind's eye and breathing naturally. Imagine yourself as you would like to look—young, beautiful, and filled with vitality. Say this affirmation three times:

*Now, I am beautiful, as I was before.*

After the affirmation, begin to chant the following spell as many times as you like, but no fewer than three:

> *Return my youth and renew my beauty that I may*
> *once again glow.*
>
> *With the power of the sun; let physical attraction*
> *in my aura show.*

After you've finished your bath and the spell, you can keep the citrine on a nightstand in your bedroom, on the vanity in the bathroom, or simply carry it to enjoy its effects.

Why did I choose three drops of frankincense and three drops of myrrh? Together they add up to the number six, which is associated with the sun in the Practical Qabalah.

Why did I choose citrine? Citrine is a solar crystal and, as such, is completely amenable to Amaterasu's energies. In the Hindu tradition, it represents the solar plexus, and in the general Western tradition it stands for the sun, the center of our inner and outer solar system. Here, you use it to create a sacred bath. Its presence is akin to having a miniature sun diffusing through the water and suffusing your body with its power. Purification, protection, and health are just a few of its benefits, not to mention physical beauty!

As a side note, myrrh is also used to clean and consecrate pearls, and frankincense is used to cleanse and consecrate topaz. If you happen to have either or both crystals, you can add them to the bath or simply dip them into the bathwater and leave them to dry. Wear them together or individually to enhance the outcome of the spell.

Another bonus: pearls are associated with yin, or feminine, energy and induce happiness and add power to feminine wiles. Blue topaz enhances psychic ability. Yellow, orange, and clear topaz crystals enhance the energies of the sun and attract admirers.

## ADDITIONAL RESOURCES

### Primary sources

Ōno Yasumaro, compiler. *The Kojiki (An Account of Ancient Matters)*, trans. Gustav Heldt (New York: Columbia University Press, 2004).

_____. *The Kojiki*, trans. Basil Hall Chamberlain (1919); for the reverse-flaying passage, see vol. I, section XV. Retrieved from *http://sacred-texts.com* (accessed 12/26/2018).

### Secondary sources

Naumann, Nelly. "*Sakahagi*: The 'Reverse Flaying' of the Heavenly Piebald Horse," *Asian Folklore Studies* 41 (1982), pp. 7–38. Thanks for the reference to Sara Thal, at the University of Wisconsin, Madison.

### NOTES

1  This paragraph is based on the work of Naumann, 1982.

# Chapter 15

# THE WISE HORSE

The horse has historically been a symbol of wisdom throughout the world and in many different cultures. The Hindu deity Hayagriva and the ancient Greek mythological centaur Chiron are two examples of this. These two manifestations of Horse Spirit played important roles in their day and age and can still play an integral role in your life today. They inspired art and sacred literature and were both revered as teachers of multiple disciplines. You can petition Hayagriva to learn how to meditate and enter a trance state. You can petition Chiron, whose gifts were so precious that he was sought out by the ancient Greek god Asclepius, for help with medical problems or even to hone your skills in hunting.

## Hayagriva

Hayagriva, which means "horse neck" in Sanskrit, is one of the many avatars of the Hindu deity Vishnu in the Vaishnavistic (Vishnu-centered) tradition. In this incarnation, Vishnu has the body of a man and the head of a pure white horse. In art, he is depicted wearing resplendent white garments and seated on a white lotus. He has four arms. One hand makes a mudra, or gesture of teaching, in which he touches thumb to forefinger. It is also a directive for patience, a recognition that there is much to learn to raise the mind beyond the mundane. In his other hands, Vishnu holds three symbolic items: the *shankha* conch shell,

Panchajanya, which is sounded as a call to prayer and used as a vessel to pour out lustral, cleansing waters; a chakra wheel with 108 blades, symbolic of the transformational energy he offers to help worshippers avoid straying from *dharma*, the path for virtuous living; and a book with sacred texts.

In one of the great Hindu compilations of sacred myths and prayers, the *Bhagavata Purana*, Vishnu takes on the form of Hayagriva during the creation of the world. In this myth, he is awakened from a deep, meditative state to learn that two demons have stolen the *Vedas*, holy literature, from the god Brahma. He successfully retrieves them, slays the thieves, and returns the books to Brahma. One Sakta-based myth tells that, during the creation, Vishnu compiled the *Vedas* in the Hayagriva avatar. Hayagriva is associated with the sun and is said to ride a solar chariot into the sky, bringing light every day. Worship of him is particularly efficacious on the full moon in August.

# SPELL TO ENHANCE FOCUS AND CONCENTRATION

Appeal to Hayagriva, the horse-neck god, to enhance your focus and concentration. This ancient Hindu deity bestows knowledge and wisdom on those who undertake studies, whether sacred or secular.

### What you need:
Essential oil of wisteria, an oil diffuser, and one yellow candle (any size).

### Instructions:
Burn the essential oil of wisteria in the oil diffuser as an offering to Hayagriva. Light the yellow candle. Concentrate on its flame while you chant the following spell at least six or nine times:

*Concentration, memory—*

*I remember all I see.*

*Answers now directly fed*

*Fall easily into my head;*

*Intelligence gives me the key,*

*Every test passed easily.*

*Hawking, Tesla, da Vinci too,*

*All the knowledge that they knew.*

*Hayagriva, river of wisdom*

*Flowing through my nervous system,*

*A genius now make of me,*

*And as my will so mote it be.*

Why did I choose wisteria? The magickal properties of wisteria enhance memory, focus, and concentration—the three building blocks of a strong intellect and psychic ability.

Why did I choose a yellow candle? Yellow and its complimentary color, violet, represent the element most closely associated to the intellect—air.

## Chiron, Immortal Centaur

The zodiacal centaur we know today as Sagittarius derives from the ancient Greek myth of Chiron, half-brother to Zeus. Because he was the son of the Titan Kronos, Chiron was immortal. By contrast, the race of mortal centaurs came from the union of Ixion, king of the Lapiths, and Nephele, who took the form of a cloud during the sexual act. Chiron's appearance in art clearly demonstrates his unique status among the centaurs. Rather than having a human torso on a horse's body, as is the norm for mortal centaurs, Chiron is shown on ancient Greek vases and sculpture with a full human body and only a horse's back and hind legs.

Chiron was not only the eldest centaur; he was also the wisest. The gods Apollo and Artemis educated him, and he was renowned for his multifaceted intellect. He was as well-versed in medicine as in the arts, and his skills in hunting and weaponry were unparalleled. His most renowned student was Achilles, the main character in Homer's *Iliad*. He also schooled a host of other prominent figures from ancient Greek mythology, including Asclepius, the god of medicine. Chiron was no cruel taskmaster, however, and the Greek poet Pindar describes him as kind.[1] In one anecdote, Achilles' mother, Thetis, looks on with jealousy as her son chooses to sleep with his arms entwined about Chiron rather than with her.

Chiron left a lasting impression on Achilles. In a poem by Statius, Achilles says that the centaur filled him with the concept of divine justice.[2] Chiron's relationship with Achilles was described by the ancient Greeks and Romans as paternal and loving. Philostratus the Elder makes this clear in his book on ancient paintings.[3] According to him, there was an image of the education of Achilles in Chiron's cave on Mount Pelion, in Thessaly. In it, the child Achilles rides Chiron, who is instructing him in horsemanship. The artist captured a crucial moment when Chiron turns to speak to the child. Achilles begins to laugh with glee as Chiron suddenly picks up his pace and turns to his pupil to say that he is controlling himself to give Achilles a gentle ride, unlike the horses who will draw his chariot one day in the Trojan War. This prophesy is perhaps the reason that Chiron was also known to have taught soothsaying.

In the end, Chiron suffered a bittersweet fate. Despite being immortal, he was not impervious to suffering, and he was inflicted with a wound he could not cure. This came to pass through his ill-fated friendship with Hercules. The myth describes how, one day, Hercules, the strongest man alive, approached Chiron out of love and, out of reverence for the god Pan, had sex with him in his cave on Mount Pelion.[4] Later, Hercules inadvertently cut the centaur with an arrow that had been dipped in the Hydra's venom. So terrible was the pain that Zeus took pity on Chiron and turned him into the constellation Centaurus.

In the context of this myth, it is not surprising that Chiron is often invoked to ensure a correct medical diagnosis.

# SPELL FOR A CORRECT MEDICAL DIAGNOSIS

For this spell, you will first invoke Chiron using the Chiron conjuration, then call on his help using the Chiron in the Sky chant.

### *What you need:*
A fresh celery leaf as an offering to Chiron (cut the leaves from a bunch you buy at the local market), one white votive candle, one deep-green votive candle, a shallow Pyrex bowl, and a quarter cup of water.

### *Instructions:*
Pour the water into the bowl and add the celery leaves. Place the two votive candles in the same bowl. The candles may touch one another. Light the white candle first, the deep-green candle second. Say the Chiron conjuration once:

> *Chiron, immortal font of compassion,*
>
> *Constellation of relief and knowledge shining in the night sky above,*
>
> *Teacher of Asclepius, the God of Medicine,*
>
> *With all the power in me and with all my heart and soul,*
>
> *I conjure, command, and invoke all your powers and energies.*

Light the white votive candle with absolute confidence that Chiron will do your bidding, and say:

> *This white flame represents the correct medical diagnosis that I seek for myself [if you are doing this on someone else's behalf, state their name here].*

Light the green votive with the same confidence that you felt while lighting the white votive, and say:

> *This green flame represents the health of mind, body, and soul that will be a natural by-product of a correct medical diagnosis for myself [if you are doing this on someone else's behalf, state their name here].*

Then repeat the Chiron in the Sky chant three, six, or nine times:

> *Chiron, star in the sky, shoot your arrow on the by and by;*
>
> *Successfully target illness unknown, its true nature must be shown.*
>
> *Within four elements now I stand, their correct combination I demand.*
>
> *Caterpillar, butterfly, chrysalis, bee, I channel all your energies now through me.*
>
> *Health I demand, therefore health I have found; great Chiron, hale in my heart we are bound.*

Let the candles burn out naturally. Drain the water, then discard the melted wax and celery leaves into the trash.

Why did I choose celery for this spell? There is a temple dedicated to the god Asclepius on the island of Sicily in the town of Selinunte (ancient Greek for "wild celery"). Here, the ill ate celery and then slept on the temple steps and grounds hoping for a dream that would lead them to the physician or medicine that would ultimately heal them.

Why did I choose a white votive? In magick, white is traditionally associated with purity and the "highest intent." Also, in this particular spell, its neutrality gives the ability to associate it with the correct medical diagnosis.

Why did I choose a deep-green votive? Deep green is associated with wealth, abundance, great health, vitality, and a strong immune system. In this particular spell, it is used to represent peace and health of mind, body, and soul.

## ADDITIONAL RESOURCES

For a prayer to Hayagriva, see: *Dhyana Sloka* (Verse for Meditation) by Vedanta Desika (1268–1370), trans. P. R. Ramachander. Retrieved from *http://celextel.org* (accessed 2/3/2018).

### Primary sources

Homer. *The Iliad*, trans. Caroline Alexander (London: HarperCollins, 2015).

Menon, Ramash. *Bhagavata Purana: The Holy Book of Vishnu*, 2 vols. (Calcutta, India: Rupa & Co., 2011).

Philostratus the Elder, Philostratus the Younger, and Callistratus. *Philostratus the Elder, Imagines. Philostratus the Younger, Imagines. Callistratus, Descriptions*, trans. Arthur Fairbanks (Cambridge, MA: Harvard University Press, 1931).

Pindar. *Pindar II: Nemean Odes, Isthmian Odes, Fragments*, trans. William H. Race (Cambridge, MA: Harvard University Press, 1997).

Pseudo-Eratosthenes. *The Constellations* in Theony Condos, trans. and comm. *Star Myths of the Greeks and Romans: A Sourcebook* (Containing the *Constellations* of Pseudo-Eratosthenes and the *Poetic Astronomy* of Hyginus) (Grand Rapids, MI: Phanes Press, 1997).

Statius. *Statius: Thebaid, Books 8–12. Achilleid*, trans. D. R. Shackleton Bailey (Cambridge, MA: Harvard University Press, 2004).

### Secondary sources

Babu, Sridhara D. *Hayagriva: The Horse-Headed Deity in Indian Culture* (Tirupati, India: Sri Venkateswara University, 1990).

### NOTES

1. Pindar, *Nemean Ode* 3.53
2. Statius, *Achilleid* 2, 96.
3 Philostratus the Elder, *Imagines* 2, Image 2
4. Condos, p. 79 (*Constellations* p. 40).

*Chapter 16*

# THE FOLKLORIC HORSE

Sometimes the most vivid people and creatures live only in legend. But who is to say that the stories passed down for generations about reclusive witches, mischievous pixies, brownies, imps, and rarely seen monstrous creatures are not true? Even the most erudite scholars have found over time that the most preposterous myths may have some basis in fact. Indeed, they have even solved mysteries this way.

The folklore of horses is no exception to this rule, and there are equine stories that originated among agrarian, so-called "simple" or "peasant" peoples that have captivated minds around the world. Never discount the power of a bedtime story that can entertain a child and also empower an adult. One such story is the tale of Baba Yaga.

## Baba Yaga

Deep in the darkest recesses of a vast, thorn-choked forest lies a small tract of emerald green land where the sun magickally shines, the rain is plentiful, and the crops thrive. No road leads in or out, but that does not seem to bother its resident. Her hut appears tiny from the exterior, but appearances are deceiving. It is slightly crooked, with a thatched roof, and stands on chicken legs. It has been known to move. Although she lives alone—though some say she has two sisters—this reclusive figure's barns and stables are meticulously tended. A fence of human bones capped with skulls surrounds the dwelling. This is the home of the witch Baba Yaga.

Legend claims that the dark forest home of Baba Yaga holds untold riches, and many have therefore sought her out. "You'll recognize her easily," say the unwitting mothers who send their children on quests to obtain money and wishes. "She is old beyond reckoning, with warts on her wrinkled face, a long pointy nose, sharp yellow teeth in a crooked smile, and long gray hair that sticks out in unkempt clumps from under a bright pink-and-blue polka-dotted head scarf. Her cloak is ill-woven and covered with patches, and her dress is torn to shreds. But take care not to stare at her drooping dugs or bony legs!"

Baba Yaga's mode of transport sets her apart from the other equestrian figures in this book—she rides a giant mortar that she guides with a pestle. Any tracks she leaves behind she quickly erases with a besom (broom). But horses she has in plenty. You just need to know how to find them—and how to find her. Baba Yaga is fickle. Sometimes she takes on the appearance of an alluring maiden to draw in a feckless youth. (Whether she eats the unfortunate lad or uses him for other purposes is unclear). At other times, she retains her hag form and, it is reputed, rewards even the dullest oaf with wealth beyond reckoning when he answers her questions in a manner that pleases her.

Perhaps Baba Yaga's least-appreciated possessions are her horses. We meet the horses in the old Russian folktale *Vasilisa the Fair*, in which the witch possesses three horses ridden by three knights who are her faithful servants.[1] One is brilliant white and heralds the dawn; another is blood red and brings the full light of day; the last is pitch black and cloaks the earth in night as it retires mysteriously into her hut.

The three horses and the knights who ride them represent the three aspects of the Triple Goddess—maiden, mother, and crone—with Baba Yaga representing the last. The colors, as I have discussed in my publication *Dragonflame*, symbolize the three stages of the Triple Goddess and of the moon: white for virginity; red for menstruation; and black for menopause or old age.[2] The three horses and knights also represent the passage of time and create a narrative of progression through time—from dawn, to day, to nightfall, or from childhood, through adulthood, to old age.

On the most direct level, horses, in a pre-Industrial era, were the prized possessions of those with wealth. And indeed, Baba Yaga has all the trappings of wealth: land, treasure, and—most important—knowledge. Her horses and knights act as heralds who disturb the time-space continuum by creating an opening at Baba Yaga's behest at three key moments in her daily life: prior to her return from the unknown; prior to her sleep; and prior to her departure once again into the unknown. They are like the squires who accompanied kings and queens, making her magickal royalty with the ability to control time.

Baba Yaga is seen as an archetype by witches and magicians alike who have studied her. She has become a living force in the subconscious minds of magickal practitioners and, like the horses and knights that serve her, she may show up unbidden. If you encounter her in a dream state or on the astral plane, the best plan is to listen, and acquiesce. Try to think of a knight dressed in white and riding a white steed; this will lead you to thoughts of the rising sun and dawn, symbols of enlightenment and waking on the earth plane.

Baba Yaga's energy is that of a crone. Simply stated, it's dark. She has wisdom; she is a magickal adept; she has complete leverage over anyone who is without magickal protection or, as she makes clear in the Russian folktale, "blessed." If you seek the help of this wise woman who lives alone deep in the forest, she will either give you a nearly unsurmountable task and then share her wisdom, or she will simply devour you. She is given to merciless whims that can change your life for the better—but at a huge price.

In the Russian folktale, the peasant maiden Vasilisa could never have anticipated becoming czarina, let alone known how to strategize something so unpredictable. But she ends up at Baba Yaga's house and stables by pure chance, receives a gift from the witch, and, after paying a tragic price (the loss of her family and house), becomes the wife of the czar. Ultimately, she lives happily ever after.

So if you choose to ask Baba Yaga for help or advice, it better be for something on a monumental scale and something that will alter your destiny for the better, because her magick has an inherent finality to it that is quite severe. Be prepared for the consequences.

## SPELL TO ENHANCE FORESIGHT

This spell is designed to bring you the wisdom and understanding necessary to obtain your dearest wish. You can even ask for "that which I need, but don't even know to ask for."

***What you need:***
Wisteria, lady's mantle, a large handful of jet chips or small tumbled jet, a besom and dustpan (you can use a broom instead), a mortar and pestle, and a small bowl.

***Instructions:***
Center and calm yourself. Be at peace. Say:

> *Great Baba Yaga, help me anticipate what's coming before*
> *anyone else does.*

Now, as you ponder the circumstance or question at hand (e.g., the outcome of a relationship, the performance of a particular stock, the best way to obtain a job/position/raise/etc.), begin mixing the wisteria and lady's mantle in the mortar using the pestle; continue for approximately three to five minutes. When finished, pour the mixture into the small bowl along with the jet. Use your hands to mix the jet, wisteria, and lady's mantle a bit more. This will help accustom you to its energies.

Beginning at the east and moving clockwise (deasil), sprinkle the mixture from the small bowl on the floor (the kitchen floor is best, but the floor in any room will work). Create a circle large enough so that you are able to stand in its center. Then take your besom and dustpan and step into the middle of the circle. Put the dustpan on the floor in front of you, inside the circle. Hold the besom in your right hand, bristles up, with the handle resting on the floor. Think of the circumstance or question you are considering once more and say this spell three times:

*Circling round and round again,*

*Like the earth orbiting the sun;*

*First morning, then night, then morning again,*

*I anticipate what's to come.*

When you are finished, beginning at the same point from which you started to create the circle in the east, use the besom to sweep the mixture into the dustpan, this time using a counterclockwise (widdershins) motion. Throw the mixture to Mother Earth and thank Baba Yaga. You are finished.

Why did I choose wisteria? Wisteria is associated with the element of air and of the mind. It is used to enhance the memory and intellect, and to gain insight.

Why did I choose jet? Jet is used to remove negativity and obstacles blocking insight. It is also used for protection. It is especially powerful when used in conjunction with wisteria to promote understanding and insight. It is powerful enough to banish any confusion that has settled in your subconscious that may be blocking the answer to your question(s).

Why did I choose lady's mantle? Lady's mantle connects you to Mother Earth during this spell. Its energies are protective and angelic, and enable you to better understand planet Earth's rotation and orbit around the sun, a necessity for this spell to work properly. It also makes the spell more effective.

What do the mortar and pestle represent? Other than being staple magickal tools, the mortar and pestle mirror Baba Yaga's mode of transportation.

What does the besom, or broom, represent? The besom mirrors Baba Yaga's infamous method of remaining invisible—by sweeping away her tracks!

What does the circle represent and why do I have you stand in the center of it to cast the spell? In this case, the circle is a symbol of the Earth's twenty-four-hour orbit around the sun—from dawn to sunset, and once again to dawn. You transform the circle into an astrological glyph of the sun by standing in the center. A circle with a dot in the center represents illumination.

## ADDITIONAL RESOURCES

Two important areas of equine European folklore and traditional witchcraft remain outside the scope of this study: the otherworldly pranksters responsible for tangling and braiding horses' manes, and the Gypsy use of the horse skull. On the former, see Claude Lecouteux, *The Tradition of Household Spirits: Ancestral Lore and Practices*, trans. Jon E. Graham (Rochester, VT: Inner Traditions, 2013), pp. 139–141; on the latter, see Claude Lecouteux, *Dictionary of Gypsy Mythology: Charms, Rites, and Magical Traditions of the Roma*, trans. Jon E. Graham (Rochester, VT: Inner Traditions, 2018), pp. 69–71.

### Secondary sources

Afanas'ev, A. N. *Russian Folk-Tales*, trans. Leonard A. Magnus (New York: E. P. Dutton & Company, 1916). Retrieved from *https://archive.org* (accessed 11/21/2018).

Illes, Judika. *Encyclopedia of Witchcraft: The Complete A-Z for the Entire Magical World* (London: HarperCollins, 2005).

Johns, Andreas. *Baba Yaga: The Ambiguous Mother and Witch of the Russian Folktale* (New York: Peter Lang, Inc., International Academic Publishers; First Edition edition, 2004).

## NOTES

1  Afanas'ev, 1916, p. 115.
2  Leo, 2014, p. 32.

# Chapter 17

# THE NATIVE AMERICAN HORSE

Long before the first peoples inhabited what are now the Americas, prehistoric eohippus (the Dawn Horse) roamed this portion of the globe. Eohippus evolved over time, and its descendants spread far and wide as tectonic shifts separated land masses into the continents we know now. Equids (mammals of the horse family) grazed the plains of North America from four million to a half million years ago—the Late Pleistocene period—as we know from fossil records recently discovered in the Yukon Territory in Canada. The horse became extinct in the Americas about ten thousand years ago, probably due to climatic changes: the land became akin to the tundra of Alaska.

In fact, it was Christopher Columbus who reintroduced Horse Spirit to the Americas on the Caribbean island of Hispaniola (now known as Haiti and the Dominican Republic) in 1493, bringing with him horses of Spanish stock. Domestic horses were first introduced to North America in Florida in 1538. It was the descendants of these horses that populated the Americas.

## Native American Traditions

It cannot be coincidence that the bond that formed between the indigenous people of the Americas, especially in North America, and Horse Spirit is so strong and mystical. Native Americans did not "encounter" the horse, in my opinion; rather they were reacquainted with kindred spirits whose fossils and life force fertilized, energized, and fortified the ground on which they lived for millennia. Native Americans traded for horses and tamed feral horses—mustangs—then established breeding programs. But the ensuing spiritual union between them and their horses has become nothing short of mythical.

This happened first in the American Southwest, where each tribe had a different rapport—physical and spiritual—with the horse, which they first called "elk-dog." The Cherokee and Creek, for example, preserve a sacred horse dance. On the other hand, the Shawnee, who lived in the area of the Ohio Valley, have a Horse Clan (*mseewiwomhsoomi*) whose members share the nature of this animal and, unlike the docile rabbit or turtle people, can be predisposed to the fiery and feisty temper that leads a horse to lash out and kick.[1]

There are many horse tales and myths from these diverse indigenous cultures. Among them is the forbidding Aisoyimstan, the Blackfeet people of Montana's god of snow and ice. He is completely white, wears white clothes, and rides a white horse. Blackfeet elders tell of Water Spirit, who gifted an orphan boy with the first horse.[2] The Navajo tell the story of Johano-ai, the Sun God, who carries the sun across the sky. A retelling of the myth relates that Johano-ai rides across the sky on one of five horses that were created from different crystals, shells, and minerals: turquoise, white shell, abalone, red shell, and coal. The color of the sky reflects the color of horse he chooses to mount. When Johano-ai's horses' hooves strike the ground, they create clouds of sparkling minerals (*pitistichi*); when they run, the sacred pollen that is offered to the gods rises like mist on the horizon. Holy men scatter this same pollen and sing songs to bless and protect horses.[3]

Turquoise, the stone that Native Americans often set in jewelry and ritual regalia, is associated with horses in many cultures. Judy Hall (author of *The Crystal Bible* series) relates turquoise to the horse's inherent spirit of liberty, whereas Judika Illes (author of *Encyclopedia of 5,000 Spells*) shares that it was meant to be worn or carried by those riding horses to prevent them from falling.[4] Claude Lecouteux recounts that, in ancient times, it was believed that placing turquoise in a horse's manger would protect it from inclement weather.[5] Regardless of its exact use, it is clear that turquoise was a stone of enormous power to Native American tribes, as you can see in this next spell, which draws on the powers of Johano-ai.

## TALISMAN BLESSING FROM THE SUN GOD JOHANO-AI

In this practice, you will use turquoise to call down a blessing from the sun god, Johano-ai. In it, you will create a pouch in a color corresponding to your intention. Here is a list of some intentions and their corresponding colors:

- Protection from enemies and black magick—black
- Astral travel and alignment of spinal chakras (especially the crown chakra)—white
- Self-discipline and a stronger will to live—red
- Protection for a love relationship or friendship—pink
- Health and peace of mind, body, and soul—cobalt blue
- Safe travels and safety while riding a horse—light blue
- Protection for vitality and wealth—emerald green
- Rapid career advancement—light green
- Illumination, recognition, and defeat of depression—golden yellow

- Joy, focus, and concentration—light yellow

- Increase of spirituality or psychic ability—deep purple

- Harmony, meditation—light purple

### What you need:

A piece of paper approximately two inches by six inches, a writing tool, a piece of turquoise, some cellophane tape, and a small pouch of a color that matches your intention.

### Instructions:

Fold the paper in half to create a central vertical crease and then fold it horizontally. Open it. At the center, where the creases meet, draw the astrological glyph of the sun (a circle with a dot in the center). Above the glyph, write the name "Johano-ai," and under the glyph, write your wish or intention. Now, take the piece of turquoise and roll it in the paper, sealing it with the tape. After choosing your intent, place the turquoise, wrapped in paper, in the appropriate color pouch and seal it (you can get a drawstring pouch or sew the pouch closed yourself). Hold it between your hands in a prayer position in front of your chest, where your heart chakra lies.

Imagine a white light coming down from your head, down through your neck and throat, chest, arms, wrists, hands, and into your palms, through the pouch and into the turquoise talisman. Say:

> Great sun god Johano-ai, teach me how to channel all your positive energies. Consecrate this talisman with your rays of might and power. May it shine with all your glory!

State your intent. For example:

> Grant me health and peace of mind, body, and soul.

Thank Johano-ai and tell him what you intend to do with your new blessing. For example:

> With health and peace of mind, body, and soul, I will move forward with my life and help myself and those both close and near to me. Thank you, Johano-ai, great god of the sun.

Carry the talisman on your person (especially when you go riding or when you travel), put it under or beside your bed, or do both.

## ADDITIONAL RESOURCES

I found two websites particularly useful for accessing tribal lore and myths: *www.aaanativearts.com* and *www.firstpeople.us*.

### Secondary sources

Bruchac III, Joseph. *Native American Animal Stories* (Golden, CO: Fulcrum Publishing, 1992).

Clark, La Verne Harrell. *They Sang for Horses: The Impact of the Horse on Navajo and Apache Folklore* (Boulder, CO: Arizona University Press, 2001).

GaWaNi Pony Boy. *Horse, Follow Closely: Native American Horsemanship* (Irvine, CA: Bow Tie Press, 1998).

Lecouteux, Claude. *A Lapidary of Sacred Stones: Their Magical and Medicinal Powers Based on the Earliest Sources*, trans. Jon E. Graham (Rochester, VT: Inner Traditions, 2012).

O'Donnell, James H. *Ohio's First Peoples* (Athens, OH: Ohio University Press, 2004).

Orlando, Ludovic, et al. "Recalibrating *Equus* Evolution Using the Genome Sequence of an Early Middle Pleistocene Horse," *Nature* 499 (July 4, 2013), pp. 74–78. Retrieved from *https://nature.com* (accessed 1/13/2019).

Price, Steve. *America's Wild Horses: The History of the Western Mustang* (New York: Skyhorse Publishing, 2017).

Singer, Ben. "A Brief History of the Horse in America: Horse Phylogeny and Evolution," *Canadian Geographic* (May 2005). Retrieved from *https://web.archive.org* (accessed 1/13/2019).

Vögelin, Carl F., and E. W. Vögelin. "Shawnee Name Groups," *American Anthropologist* 37 issue 4 (October–December 1935), pp. 617–635.

## NOTES

1  Vögelin, 1935, p. 628.
2  See *http://firstpeople.us.*
3  Ibid.
4  I thank Judy and Judika for sharing these insights via private communication.
5  Lecouteux, 2012, p. 323.

# Chapter 18

# THE FASHION HORSE

Hoof, mane, and velvety equine muzzle regularly grace fashion magazines and are perpetually in vogue. Why? Owning a horse and learning to ride one have long been privileges of the wealthy. This remains largely true today. The mystique and allure of hobnobbing with the rich and famous by riding in a fox hunt, attending a royal polo match, buying the right hat to attend a famous horse race, or visiting the stables behind the scenes at the Kentucky Derby are undeniable.

Designers began capitalizing on this cachet as early as 1953, when Gucci introduced the men's moccasin with a snaffle bit in metal that has since made its way onto purses and other accessories. The jockey style is connected historically to Chanel. Dior created the well-known saddlebag purse. Ferragamo, Courrèges, and Lanvin have also had their equine moments. The house of Hermès is renowned for providing luxury equipage—riding apparel like saddles and tack, as well as clothing for the ultra-rich. Ralph Lauren made his enduring claim to fame with his Polo brand, an image of a polo rider with mallet held high in pursuit of a ball—a logo that is emblazoned like modern-day heraldry on all his clothes. He also plays on the all-American spirit of the cowboy with his line called Chaps. The quintessentially English design house, Burberry, also uses an equine logo.

The grand couturiers quote endlessly from riding motifs, and models saunter down the catwalk with high veiled hats reminiscent of women riding side-saddle, jodhpurs, shining leather knee-high riding boots, and velvet riding helmets. The late, great, bad boy of fashion, Alexander McQueen, the cutting-edge deconstructionist Martin Margiela, and the flamboyant John Galliano are famous for including horses in their shows or posing on them in promotional shots. Indeed, the "fashion horse"—defined in its figurative sense as "a person whose sole function seems to be to show off clothes"—has been around since the mid-19th century and will probably never stray far from the pages of *Vogue, Vanity Fair,* and *GQ.*[1] As magickal practitioners, we can use this incarnation of Horse Spirit to bring good fortune and success to our lives.

## Paimon and Haziel

One of the most wonderful aspects of magick is that there is an opposite for every spell, rite, ritual, or pact. This holds true for magickal beings, entities, and spirits as well. To climb the ladder of success, many are drawn to the demon Paimon (as named in the *Lesser Key of Solomon,* also known as the *Goetia*). He is a grand seducer, who would draw you into a pact in which he promises to provide fame and wealth in return for your career, or perhaps something else that he considers a fair exchange for great advancement. But beware the consequences! Once entangled with Paimon's energies, it can be next to impossible to escape or break the pact. If you don't give him what he considers his just due, he will surely retaliate with a curse.

Luckily, there is another *daemon* (Latin for "spirit") with a less demanding approach to magickal pacts. His name is Haziel (Hebrew for "God sees"). Haziel—whose secret number is fifty-three in numerological traditions—appears as a young man in his late twenties or early thirties with short brown hair in loose curls. He wears a long, flowing white tunic that trails approximately ten feet behind him. He exudes holiness and wisdom, and his demeanor is simultaneously serious, compassionate, and loving.

Haziel wants us to understand that there is nothing whatsoever wrong with the desire to reach the pinnacle of success in the mundane world. This can happen in whatever field you desire, as long as your success serves a benevolent purpose. His message teaches us that there is no need to turn to darker energies to achieve this kind of success.

In a tarot deck, each of the thirty-six numbered cards, also known as pips, has an angel who presides over it by day and one who presides over it by night. Haziel is the holy entity who presides over the nine of pentacles by day.[2] The nine of pentacles indicates the arrival of good luck, money, fortune, savings, and a brilliant idea that will manifest into financial success.

## SPELL TO REACH THE PINNACLE OF SUCCESS

I created this spell to give you the ability to tap into the positive energies of the nine of pentacles through the permission of the angel Haziel. It will also automatically negate any evil, greed, curse, enemies, or unsettling energies that may have been following you under the guise of the demon Paimon.

***What you need:***
An oil diffuser, essential oil of verbena, a piece of rough rose quartz, a light-blue candle, the nine of pentacles from a traditional tarot deck, a pen and paper, and the sigil of Haziel.

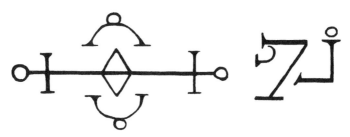

*Sigil of Haziel.*

**Instructions:**

Place the light-blue candle, the oil diffuser with verbena in it, and the rough rose quartz on your altar. Set your goal and write it on a piece of paper about three inches high and eight inches wide.

Decide in what field you want to succeed. Composing music? Acting? Modeling? Real estate? Sales? Networking? Writing? Or perhaps something totally different. It's up to you; just make sure that your intent includes a benevolent or altruistic purpose.

On the other side of the paper, trace the sigil of Haziel. (You may want to practice drawing the sigil a couple times before finally tracing it on your goal paper.) Fold the paper three times and put it under the piece of rough rose quartz. Light the oil diffuser with essential oil of verbena in it. Light the light-blue candle. Say:

> *Fifty-three! Haziel! Holy one! Whose name means "God sees." Accept my humble offerings. Teach me how to channel all your positive energies, teach me how to foster a relationship with your kind, reveal your secrets to me, and grant me that which I need that I do not even know to ask for, so that I may help myself and those both close and near to me.*

State your wish.

> *Bring me to the pinnacle of success in the field of [state your desire].*

Speak to Haziel in a heartfelt manner. The angels like to hear why you aspire to such lofty goals and what you will do once you achieve them. End by saying this affirmation three times:

> *Now, I continue to build my career around successful endeavors. So be it!*

Extinguish the candle and thank Haziel in advance.

Perform the above rite seven days in a row. Fourteen is even better. And forty days (an alchemical month) is the best to achieve strong results.

Concentrate every night on the sigil. Stare at it. Draw it until you can see it clearly in your mind's eye, without discomfort or struggle. When you call out "fifty-three," imagine the sigil emblazoned in white in your mind's eye.

After you have finished the seven-, fourteen-, or forty-day rite, burn the goal paper and blow the ashes to the wind. Keep the rough rose quartz in a special place. Repeat this rite whenever you like. Try to light the candle and perform the rite during the day—before sunset.

Because Haziel is the angel of the third quinance of Virgo (an astrological phase of five degrees), this rite is especially powerful when you perform it during the astrological month of Virgo. To add even more potency, chant Psalm 25:6 as many times as you like after saying your affirmations: "Remember, Lord, your great mercy and love, for they are from of old."

Why did I choose essential oil of verbena? Verbena, also known as vervain, is the chosen herb and fragrance of Haziel and therefore makes a suitable offering to him. It is also used to enhance magickal operations and invoke solar energies used for illumination.

Why did I choose rough rose quartz? The angel Haziel is associated with the element of earth, wealth, self-love, and forgiveness, all of which are associated with rose quartz. Rough rose quartz is a more natural, "earthy" form.

Why did I choose a light-blue candle? Light blue is associated with spirituality, lofty ideals, and peace. It is Haziel's chosen color.

## ADDITIONAL RESOURCES

*Secondary sources*

Crowley, Aleister, Hymenaeus Beta, and Samuel Liddell MacGregor Mathers, trans. and ed. *The Goetia: The Lesser Key of Solomon the King: Lemegeton—Clavicula Salomonis Regis, Book 1* (Boston: Red Wheel, 1995).

DuQuette, Lon Milo. *Tarot of Ceremonial Magick: A Pictorial Synthesis of Three Great Pillars of Magick (Astrology, Enochian Magick, Goetia)* (York Beach, ME: Samuel Weiser, Inc., 1995).

Godwin, David. *Godwin's Cabalistic Encyclopedia: Complete Guide to Both Practical and Esoteric Applications*, 3rd ed. (Woodbury, MN: Llewellyn Publications, 2003); Haziel's sigil is found on p. 138.

## NOTES

1  Retrieved from *https://etymonline.com* (accessed 1/11/2019).
2  On this subject, see DuQuette, 1995, pp. 200–201.

*Chapter 19*

# THE OLDEST HORSE

Today, travelers to Khustain Nuruu National Park, situated in the great steppes of Mongolia, can see scattered herds of dun-colored, stocky horses roaming freely, just as Johann Schiltberger did in the 1390s. It is hard to imagine, but these are truly the last wild horses in existence.

Terminology here is important. "Wild" designates the horse to which Przewalski (*shuh-val-ski*) gave his name as a *species* in the late 19th century. This horse was related to the Botai culture, which may have first domesticated the horse, as we saw in chapter 3. It does not designate a *breed* that has gone feral, like the American mustang. Mustangs were not native to the Americas, but are descendants of horses the Spanish brought in the 15th century, as discussed in chapter 17. In fact, by then, eohippus had been extinct in this area for millennia (see chapter 2). Over the fifty years following Przewalski's identification of this Mongolian horse, it became extinct in the wild and was only saved by breeding examples that were found in zoos. But there is a twist! Although the Botai culture did not last, their horses certainly did, as geneticists have now proven.[1] They lived in the wild for almost 4,000 years before being rediscovered.

The horse played a key role in the life of the Mongols and it is sacred in their mythology with associations to the creator and the solar deity, Ülgen. He, it was believed, provided abundance and protection to his faithful, but he demanded the sacrifice of a white horse as part of his worship. This was accomplished by shamans who participated in complex rituals involving trances and travel into the spirit world where they could gain secret knowledge about the well-being of the people.

By honoring Ülgen with the sacrifice of a horse, the Mongols sought to bring abundance, justice, and protection to their communities. Would that we should seek the same! There is so much social injustice in our lives today that it is nearly impossible for our true selves to emerge. Our true selves are threatened with extinction, just like Przewalski's horse. This is especially true when we enter a new environment—a new job, a new social setting, or a new school. It can be difficult to make your voice heard.

But I keep a small light burning deep inside me—a vision of an ideal future, if you will, in which all people are treated equally within their diversity. In the distant future, the human race will most likely become a new species—cyborg. Perhaps we will be living in round "studio apartments" that orbit the Earth. Perhaps we will be downloading knowledge from sources as different as traditional languages and birdsong directly into our brains. Perhaps we will finally grasp artificial intelligence and astral travel enough to use both to enhance the quality of our lives. Because we desire instant gratification, perhaps we will eventually become telepathic.

As appealing as this vision of the future may be, however, for now, we must live in the present. But we can improve that present by beginning to accept one another's differences as beautiful, right now! How else will we survive peacefully in the distant future?

## SPELL TO EMBRACE YOUR UNIQUENESS

This spell is designed to help you to embrace your own "fierce" self—the truly wild horse within you. But you can do that only by embracing your uniqueness. Accept yourself. Accept yourself with confidence. Accept yourself with confidence and courage. Do this and you are destined to be a leader or a pioneer.

**What you need:**
A titanium aura quartz crystal.

**Instructions:**
Hold your hands in prayer position with the titanium aura quartz crystal between them in front of your heart chakra. Imagine Ülgen's bright, golden light pouring through your body as you chant the uniqueness spell:

> *Ülgen, send your light to me,*
> *Bright and strong for all to see.*
> *Of flesh and blood I am built.*
>
> *On this planet's axis tilt—*
>
> *Straight, curved, serpentine—*
> *I fit perfectly, not in between.*
>
> *Ülgen, send your light to bless;*
>
> *I proudly own my U-Nique-Ness.*

Why did I choose a titanium aura quartz crystal? Titanium aura quartz is an alchemical blend of clear quartz with titanium and gold. It has a futuristic quality and is neither masculine nor feminine. Its magickal associations include joy and psychic ability. This stone will protect your own personal transformation and evolution. It will enhance your inner strength and courage and pride, allowing your true self to emerge.

### ADDITIONAL RESOURCES

For images of and general information on Przewalski's horse, see: *https://arkive.org.*

**Primary sources**
Schiltberger, Johannes. *Hans Schiltbergers Reisebuch nach der Nürnberger Handschrift*, ed. Valentin Langmantel (Tübingen,

Germany 1885). This 14th-century, eyewitness account is available in full on *https://archive.org*.

### Secondary sources

Boyd, Lee, and Katherine A. Houpt, ed. *Przewalski's Horse: The History and Biology of an Endangered Species* (Albany, NY: State University of New York Press, 1994). Although certain parts of this book have been superseded by advances in science and archaeology, it remains an important source of information with contributions from multiple disciplines.

Gaunitz, C., et al. "Ancient Genomes Revisit the Ancestry of Domestic and Przewalski's Horses," *Science Magazine* 360 (6384) (April 6, 2018), pp. 111–114.

Jansen, Thomas, et al. "Mitochondrial DNA and the Origins of the Domestic Horse," *Proceedings of the National Academy of Sciences of the United States of America* 99.16 (2002), pp. 10905–10910.

## NOTES

1   Gaunitz, 2018.

*Chapter 20*

# THE TRIUMPHANT HORSE

Magick manifests spontaneously and we always need to be ready to recognize and receive it. On a recent trip, I visited the tomb of Marie Laveau (1801–1881), the mysterious Voodoo Queen of New Orleans. Just before I returned home, a magickal message came to me in the form of a story from an elderly Uber driver.

"The airport please," I said, as I got in the car. It was the end of a wonderful trip, but I had time to kill and the driver had stories to tell.

"You have a lot of time before your flight leaves," he said. "And I've lived here all my life. That's over sixty-some years. Do you want me to tell you a story? It was told to me by my grandmother, who learned it from her grandmother. I can even show you where it happened."

Without hesitation I answered: "Absolutely!"

The story was bone-chilling.

## Marie Laveau and the Five Black Horses

Once there was a white slave owner who was notorious for her cruelty. She had five black slaves—all males. If she felt one needed to be disciplined, even on a whim, she shackled all five to an iron cross leaning on its side. The cross was a traditional Christian cross, but it was pushed over, with one arm stuck in the ground. This eerie torture device—something holy that was defiled by this woman—held true to its symbolic meaning of suffering.

The slave owner had had an ironsmith attach five pairs of shackles along the arms of this cross, and when she needed to use it for discipline, she herself shackled each of the five slaves to it. She contorted their bodies, placing one hand in a shackle near the ground and another hand in a shackle toward the top of the cross, almost pulling joints out of their sockets. Sometimes she would twist their arms as if they were in a straitjacket, pulling the left arm over right or the right over the left. When she was finished, all five slaves were cuffed in the five pairs of shackles—twisted, nude, and gagged. All anyone heard were guttural moans, and no one could do anything to help for fear they would be killed.

But the spirits who watched over the slaves had power, too. The legend goes that, at night when everyone was asleep, the slaves turned into black horses—powerful with bloodlust and seeking vengeance for their mistreatment. Together, they chose a local slave owner to trample, kick, and bite to death. In the morning, their owner found the five men still shackled as if they had never left the cross—but covered with blood, sweat, and dirt.

Finally, one evening, the five slaves chose their owner as the object of their revenge. She was found the next day, shackled to the same cross on which she had punished them, with her head crushed; there were hoof prints embedded in her chest and pieces of flesh had been bitten from her body. As members of her household took her down from the same cross she had used to punish her slaves, no one wept. It was a closed-casket funeral.

Today, people still pray to Marie Laveau to exact vengeance in a karmically correct manner. They ask her to send the five black horses of the night as arbiters of justice, especially in the face of discrimination and racism.

*Marie Laveau's five black horses.*

# SPELL FOR JUSTICE AND
# TO END DISCRIMINATION

Voodoo Queen Marie Laveau's iconic status and power still exist on the astral realm. Her energy waits for your call for help. You can invoke that energy with the following spell and use it to build or reestablish your self-esteem, lift yourself up, or maintain your strength in difficult situations. Most important, this spell can protect you and others from injustice and counter any attempts to discriminate against you and others. Use it to gain equality for yourself and to help others. It only takes one voice to change history!

***What you need:***

Three peach moonstones.

***Instructions:***

At midnight, go outside. Under the night sky, hold the three moonstones in your hand and think of the person or people who wish to harm you. Ask Marie Laveau to come to your aid. As an offering to her, throw the moonstones among flowers, or simply to the ground. If you can, go to New Orleans and place the three peach moonstones at the foot of her tombstone. Alternately, you can place them on rose petals on your altar before a picture of her as if you were placing them at her tomb. (You can easily find famous paintings of Laveau on the Internet.) Recite the following spell as many times as you wish. As you do so, imagine your enemies and all their hatred and desire to hurt you wasting away to nothing:

> *You pull my tail, you twist my mane;*
> *I'll play along, you'll think I'm lame.*
>
> *You'd brand oppression on my destiny's scroll,*
> *But your action's void; no one owns my soul.*
>
> *You've gone too far, you are a piece of waste;*
>
> *The sky will fall, you'll be crushed by disgrace.*
> *I'm the dark, dark horse that won the race.*
>
> *All the grief was a gift, raising me higher;*
> *All your hatred made a forge for my crystal fire.*
>
> *Marie Laveau, Voodoo Queen,*
> *Set all aright with magick unseen.*
>
> *Three moonstones peach I leave at your tomb;*
> *Where once there was war, now flowers bloom.*

Why did I choose peach moonstones? Moonstone catches the qualities of the moon. It is also known to quell angst, and to draw out hatred from a black or bitter heart. The peach hue and glimmer are important, because they capture and reflect the warmth of the heart of the high priestess of Voodoo, Marie Laveau.

Why did I choose *three* peach moonstones? The number three is associated with the Qabalistic energy source of the Great Mother, whose powers bind and give shape to an otherwise chaotic force of shapeless potential, sometimes in a way that we may consider violent.

*Cameo portrait of Voodoo Queen Marie Laveau.*

## ADDITIONAL RESOURCES

### Secondary sources

Alvarado, Denise. *The Magic of Marie Laveau: Embracing the Spiritual Legacy of the Voodoo Queen of New Orleans* (Newburyport, MA: Weiser Books, 2019).

Long, Carolyn Morrow. *A New Orleans Voudou Priestess: The Legend and Reality of Marie Laveau* (Gainesville, FL: University Press of Florida, 2006).

Ward, Martha. *Voodoo Queen: The Spirited Lives of Marie Laveau* (Oxford, Mississippi: University Press of Mississippi, 2004).

*Chapter 21*

# THE APOCALYPTIC HORSE

Who will hear the final scrape of an impatient horse's hoof or the last pounding thuds of a galloping herd? The powerful imagery of the four horsemen who usher in the messages foretelling the end of time in the *Apocalypse of John* has captivated sinners and saints since the time it was written. "When the sun goes black, the moon turns red, the stars fall from the sky, and the earth shakes violently," John writes, "the end of time and the final judgment of God are at hand" [Rev. 6].

## The Four Horsemen of the Apocalypse

"Apocalypse" is the Greek word for the Latin word for "revelation"—the name of the book placed at the end of the Bible. John—not to be confused with the author of the Gospel of John—received these visions, which were meant to give comfort at the time he wrote of them, likely under the persecution of Christians during the reigns of Roman Emperors Domitian (b. 51, r. 81–96 CE) and Nero (b. 37, r. 54–68 CE).

In his vision, John sees four symbolic horses: a white horse whose rider holds a bow and arrow; a red horse whose rider holds a huge sword; a black horse whose rider holds a pair of scales; and a pale horse named Death, "with Hades following at its heels." Many famous theologians and seers have proposed a bewildering range of esoteric interpretations of this vision, but none so intriguing as that of American psychic and author Edgar Cayce (1877–1945). His own visions concerning this biblical text reveal that it does not relate to the end of the world or a series of events, but rather preserves an encrypted message for human transformation.

For Cayce, the *Apocalypse* is a complex metaphor that applies to the next stage of human evolution—the end of *homo sapiens.* (The evolutionary change that ushered in *homo sapiens* took place around 300,000 years ago with the relative decline and extinction of *homo erectus* and *homo Heidelbergensis.*) In the next stage of evolution, Cayce predicts revolutionary alterations for all physical and spiritual components of the body, and he interprets the four horsemen as part of this monumental change. Specifically, he claims they stand for the four animal emotions that humanity will need to conquer and control in order for this transformation to take place. He envisions the opening of all chakras, or energy centers, in the human body, which will permit a mental awakening. This will, in turn, lead to a spiritual and psychic awakening.

Edgar Cayce interpreted the *Apocalypse* in his role as a psychic. In that same role, I believe and predict that the gift of telepathy—mental communication—is part of the dynamic process he describes. One of the greatest motivators for this transformation to take place can be summed up in one sentence: It's faster for humans to communicate telepathically. This desire alone, which is subconscious in people throughout the world, will eventually catapult humankind into their next stage of development. This spell builds on Cayce's interpretation of the *Apocalypse,* but emphasizes heightened speed for personal evolution.

# SPELL FOR TELEPATHIC EVOLUTION

For this spell, I choose to invoke Kali, the Hindu Goddess of destruction and rebirth, and the fourth "pale" horse from the *Apocalypse*, which symbolizes death. These two powerful forces work with the central "nervous system" that controls all four levels of existence—physical, emotional, mental, and spiritual. Working with them can bring you into an unknown, yet anticipated, fifth level of existence—one in which humans will be able to communicate telepathically.

Kundalini, the great and secret serpent that is coiled at the base of the spine, is the spark of life in human and animal matter. Humans can "force" it to rise through the seven main chakras, breaking the "seal" of each, to help us evolve. Cayce parallels this to the biblical description of an angel opening the seals on a book. The outcome may include mind-reading, enhanced psychic ability, astral travel, and an understanding that there are more than three dimensions.

***What you need:***
A calm and open mind.

***Instructions:***
Sit in a comfortable position in your favorite chair. Enter into silent meditation for a short period of time. Now bring your attention to your mind's eye. Try to live within your mind's eye by imagining your entire physical body present in the area known as the brow chakra. Try to lose the sensation of the outline of your physical body and what you are sitting on. Now bring the sensation of your physical body into the brow chakra.

Begin to visualize a golden orb (known as the Self in psychology and philosophy). Sit at its center. Open yourself to the possibility of evolving into the next stage of humanity. Leave this as defined or as ambiguous as you like.

Come out of the silence. Recite the following spell with conviction, using this holy and powerful Sanskrit mantra: *Om Kali Ma*. It banishes negativity on all levels, leaving room for the next stage of your development to occur:

> *Great Mother Kali, goddess of destruction and rebirth, I call on your energies.*
>
> *Ride to me on the fourth horse of the Apocalypse, which is pale as death.*
>
> *I am not afraid! Destroy my old self and disperse my ego, and I will be reborn.*
>
> *I seek to experience truth beyond human ego—*
> *Om Kali Ma!*
>
> *Chi, pure energy, break the seal of my root chakra—*
> *Om Kali Ma!*
>
> *Chi, pure energy, break the seal of my sacral chakra—*
> *Om Kali Ma!*
>
> *Chi, pure energy, break the seal of my solar plexus chakra—*
> *Om Kali Ma!*
>
> *Chi, pure energy, break the seal of my heart chakra—*
> *Om Kali Ma!*
>
> *Chi, pure energy, break the seal of my throat chakra—*
> *Om Kali Ma!*
>
> *Chi, pure energy, break the seal of my brow chakra—*
> *Om Kali Ma!*
>
> *Chi, pure energy, break the seal of my crown chakra—*
> *Om Kali Ma!*
>
> *Kundalini, Great and Secret Serpent, Rise!*
>
> *It is time for the next stage, a new age—*
> *Om Kali Ma!*

# ADDITIONAL RESOURCES

*Secondary sources*

Cayce, Edgar. *The Book of the Revelation: A Commentary Based on a Study of Twenty-Three Psychic Discourses by Edgar Cayce* (Virginia Beach, VA: A. R. E. Press, 1969).

Todeschi, Kevin J. *Edgar Cayce on Soul Symbolism: Creating Life Seals, Aura Charts, and Understanding the Revelation* (Virginia Beach, VA: Yazdan Publishing, 2015).

Van Auken, John. *Edgar Cayce on the Revelation: A Study Guide for Spiritualizing Body and Mind* (New York: Sterling, 2005).

*Chapter 22*

# SPELLS-ON-THE-RUN

The beauty of magick is the thunderbolt that inspires it—the lightning that rouses the spirit to action. The French have captured this powerful and romantic concept in the elegant phrase *coup de foudre*, which means "stroke of lightning." They use the phrase to describe love at first sight. Thunderbolt, love, inspiration—these are some of magick's most salient and motivational underpinnings, as well as some of life's most precious jewels.

This chapter gives you nine easy-to-use, but nonetheless powerful, spells that can draw down that thunderbolt to inform your magic when time is of the essence. They are all inspired by idioms and proverbs that center around horses. All you need to perform them is a rock or crystal, a regular playing card and/or a card from a tarot deck, and a candle (although occasionally an extra item or two may be suggested).

Before you begin one of these spells, please read it through entirely. I have designed them in simple form, but you will find that each offers challenges at its core—investigating your motives, defining your agenda, and setting your moral compass. Each is followed by helpful information that you can learn from and use in your future magickal work.

Fears and worries are often at the root of problems you are trying to resolve—like weeds slowly strangling nearby healthy plants. These nine spells can help you weed out some of these fears and worries by showing you how to pull them up by the roots. First, ask yourself why you need to perform a particular spell. By defining your goal, setting your purpose, and realizing that some type of sacrifice is necessary (e.g., time and/or energy), you will deepen your understanding of your true motivations, and ultimately your true Self. (To learn more about this process, see my book *Dragonflame*.)

Most of these spells involve working with lit candles. They may also require placing the candles on top of a tarot card, a regular playing card, or a piece of paper. Always remember to be careful when working with fire. I suggest placing candle(s) in a flat, shallow bowl filled with a small amount of water and setting the bowl on a heat-resistant trivet. The spells will still work if you place the trivet and bowl on top of the cards or piece of paper, rather than directly on a flammable surface.

## BETTING ON THE WRONG HORSE

How many times have you picked the wrong person as an employee, or for love, or for babysitting, or to fix your car? We all make decisions all day, every day. When you fear you're about to make a wrong decision, this spell can help you avoid choosing the wrong person—for any purpose—and keep you headed in the right direction.

**What you need:**
A white candle (taper or votive), the Knight of Cups card from a tarot deck, and a piece of citrine.

**Instructions:**
Place the Knight of Cups card centered in the middle of your altar. Place the white candle to the right of it. Place the citrine to the right of the candle. While thinking of your decision, gently place your right hand on the Knight of Cups and say:

> *I give you my dilemma. Is it a good or bad decision to [state the issue]?*

Light the white candle and say:

> *Knight of Cups, carry my decision through the flame of discernment and leave only the truth behind.*

Put your right hand over the citrine and say:

> *I give you permission to change my mind, so I make the correct decision.*

Let the candle burn out naturally. When the wax remnants are cooled, throw them in the trash. Leave the Knight of Cups and the citrine on your altar until you receive an answer. Once you do, thank the Knight of Cups as you put it back into the tarot deck. Gift the citrine to a person you feel needs it.

Why did I choose the Knight of Cups? In this spell, the Knight of Cups becomes the warden of your decision-making process. You are giving it permission to carry your decision through the flame of discernment as represented by the white candle. In this way, the dross and confusion will be burned away, leaving only the truth as represented by the citrine. The Knight of Cups often represents an invitation, or an opportunity. It also signals the element of water, water elementals (undines), emotions, and the astrological sign of Cancer. This knight's armor is not hiding rust in its interior. There is no deception, only a heartfelt desire to help you find the truth.

Why did I choose a white candle? White connotes purity, cleansing, and clarity.

Why did I choose citrine? Citrine is known for its solar properties of illumination and health. In this spell, it sheds light on the truth and may bring you a message concerning your decision in a dream or spontaneous illumination.

# CHARLEY HORSE

This spell is used mainly to break a curse, ward off black magick, block the evil eye, and protect from psychic attacks. But it can also be used to stop your enemies from getting ahead and to delay an event or business meeting. If you wake up with anxiety, or if there have been one too many negative incidents befalling you lately, or if you simply want to protect yourself from negative energies, then this spell is for you.

### What you need:

A piece of clear quartz with a point sharp enough to carve wax, and one white candle (taper or votive).

### Instructions:

Carve the number sixty-one (61) into one side of the candle. Carve a circle inside a circle on the other side to represent the evil eye. (Remember, it's the intention, not the artistic ability, that counts.) Put the candle in the middle and center of your altar and say:

> Now, I stand in a ring of fire that no person, spirit, entity, energy, or thought form can cross except those that have my best interests at heart.

Light the candle and say:

> I banish all evil, evil eyes, curses, negativity, upset conditions, black magick, psychic attacks, and opposition. Go back from whence you came—now! So be it!

Let the candle burn out naturally and throw away the cooled remnants of wax. You can repeat this spell as often as you like, but it is especially powerful on the new and full moons.

Why did I choose a white candle? White represents nothingness within this spell. It connotes an impenetrable wall of white light that banishes all evil. White is connected to the highest and loftiest energies of our inner and outer universe.

Why did I choose the symbol of the evil eye? In this spell, and in general, it is used as an apotropaic—an amulet or symbol to ward off evil and black magick.

Why did I choose the number sixty-one? Sixty-one is based on Hebrew *gematria,* a system used to analyze words, names, and phrases by assigning each letter of the alphabet a numerical value. The sums of words, names, and phrases that match in numerical value hold a magickal energy or power in relationship to one another. In Hebrew, the number sixty-one holds the same numerical value as the word that means "nothing." This number was chosen with great care to be used in this spell. Its energy annihilates everything, turning all evil that comes toward it into nothingness.

# GET OFF YOUR HIGH HORSE

This spell is used to break your own ego or that of another, to put someone in his or her place, to even the playing field, and to banish enmity. If someone's negative actions cause you to "lose your voice," or if your own actions are hurting you, or if you know someone who needs to be taught a lesson, this spell is for you.

**What you need:**
A red candle (taper or votive) and any needle sharp enough to carve into wax.

**Instructions:**
Carve the first and last name of the person you feel is causing problems up the side of the candle, starting at the bottom and heading toward the wick. (If you don't know the person's last name, the spell will still work.) Place the candle in the middle and center of your altar. Light it and say this spell three times (not two or four, but three):

> *A sharp needle's words of advice:*
> *As you sew your destiny think twice.*
> *If you slip, your finger may smart*
> *But karma is a sword through your heart.*

Let the candle burn out naturally and throw the remnants of cooled wax in the trash.

Why did I choose a red candle? Red is associated with passion, power, and blood. In this spell, its color is used to symbolize a fiery and imminent warning.

Why did I choose three times for this spell to be chanted? The number three symbolizes the women associated with the power behind this spell: the Triple Goddess, the three Fates, and the three Weird Sisters. All represent the inevitable, that which can be changed only with great effort, magick, and foresight! Three is a number of binding and of destiny.

This spell is based on the three Fates: destiny, inevitability, and fortune. It is also based on the Weird Sisters, the three witches from William Shakespeare's play *Macbeth*. Its power is found in this truth: Think twice; all words and deeds have consequences. Some are slightly painful—like a pinprick—while others are irreversibly devastating—like a sword through the heart. The energy of this spell acts as a warning to the person targeted. Poor Macbeth! He was warned by the Weird Sisters; if only he hadn't allowed his ego to blind him!

## LOOSING UNBRIDLED PASSION

This spell is used to create an uncontrollable sexual urge in someone, to enhance physical attraction, and to create a romantic connection. If someone new has entered your life and you feel an instant connection but aren't sure it is shared—and if you would like to explore the possibility of a sexual relationship with that person—then this spell is for you.

### *What you need:*
A small decorative bowl, one tumbled piece of carnelian, one tumbled piece of rose quartz, one tumbled piece of clear quartz, two cinnamon sticks, one red taper candle, and one pink taper candle (both candles should be the same size).

**Instructions:**

Place the bowl in the middle and center of your altar. Place the candles just above the bowl. Put the carnelian, rose quartz, and clear quartz crystals in the bowl. Put the cinnamon sticks over them in the shape of an "X." Then say:

> Give [name of intended recipient] an uncontrollable urge to
> have sex with me. Remove all obstacles that hinder us from
> being together. Let this be a starting point, a romantic connec-
> tion that would otherwise not have been.

Light the red and pink candles. As you light them, think of the recipient and say:

> Make me happy.

After they are both lit, say:

> With all the power in me and with all my heart and soul
> I, [name/magickal name], hereby send physical attraction
> and love with every beat of my heart to [name of intended
> recipient].

Take a few moments to imagine the energy of physical attraction being sent to your recipient. Conjure an emotion of romance and love. When you feel you are finished, thank the spirits in advance. Let the candles burn out naturally and throw the remnants of cooled wax in the trash. Keep the bowl and its ingredients on your altar.

Why did I choose carnelian, rose quartz, and clear quartz? When carnelian and rose quartz are used in combination, they create a strong foundation for a love relationship. Carnelian is associated with carnal desires. Rose quartz is associated with love and friendship. Clear quartz enhances the magickal associations of the carnelian and rose quartz and creates clarity of intent.

Why did I choose cinnamon sticks? Cinnamon is associated with success and love. By placing the cinnamon sticks in the shape of an "X," you magickally combine your energies with the recipient's energies.

Why did I choose pink and red candles? Pink and red are powerful together. They represent the fusion of love and physical attraction—the two ingredients necessary to start a successful love relationship.

# REKINDLING THE FLAME

This spell is used to reignite your sex life and to banish inhibitions. If your sex life has been on the rocks for a while, or perhaps is even non-existent, or if inhibitions are holding you back from enjoying a fulfilling sex life, then this spell is for you.

***What you need:***
A fireproof plate, cinnamon, and a red taper candle.

***Instructions:***
Put the plate in the middle and center of your altar. Center the red candle on the plate and light it. Say:

> *As this candle burns, so does my sex life.*

Sprinkle a dash of cinnamon over the flame and candle, then say:

> *Sparks of life, sparks of passion, come into my life and cause a reaction.*

Sprinkle another dash, then say:

> *Sparks of passion, sparks of life, remove all inhibitions, remove all strife.*

Let the candle burn out naturally. When the wax remnants have cooled, throw them in the trash.

Why did I choose a red candle? In magick, the color red is associated with desire, strength, intense emotions, passion, sex, and lust.

Why did I choose cinnamon? The magickal associations of cinnamon are success, love, and good luck. It can also be used in conjunction with fire, or as an incense, to evoke a sense of zest and zeal that removes mild hindrances and inhibitions.

# STRONG AS A HORSE

This spell is used to create and enhance fortitude, to help you stand your ground, to induce stalwart energy, and to help you stand by your decisions. If you need an extra dosage of courage or physical strength, then this spell is for you.

**What you need:**
The Strength card from a tarot deck (in some tarot decks, this card is number eight; in others it is number eleven), an emerald-green candle (taper or votive), and a piece of tumbled tiger's-eye.

**Instructions:**
Place the candle in the middle and center of your altar and light it. Place the Strength card in front of the candle and put the tiger's-eye on top of it. Let the candle burn out naturally. When the wax remnants have cooled, throw them in the trash. Put the Strength card back into the tarot deck. Wear or carry the tiger's-eye.

Why did I choose an emerald-green candle? Emerald green, or deep green, is associated with the endless cycle of life, death, and rebirth—fecundity, abundance, and vital energies.

Why did I choose a tiger's-eye? Tiger's-eye is associated with courage and strength. It attracts spirits of endurance from the astral realm.

Why did I choose the Strength card? Strength gives access to the spirits of knowledge and bravery, two skills that impart power. Knowledge relieves helplessness; bravery relieves fear. The Strength card usually bears an image of a woman taming a lion. In this spell, its energies will tame your inner lion, allowing you to use its strength at will and perform at your highest capacity.

# HOLD YOUR HORSES

This spell is used to set boundaries, manage impulse control, and temper anger. It can help you think before speaking, make healthy and thoughtful decisions, and communicate clearly and concisely. If you are having trouble keeping a secret, this spell is for you. If it seems you are always in a rush, especially to make it to a meeting or social gathering on time, this spell is for you.

*What you need:*
A blank piece of paper, something to write with, the Chariot card from a tarot deck, and a gray candle (taper or votive).

*Instructions:*
At middle and center of the paper, write your target goal, a personal attribute that you want to enhance—for example, setting boundaries, managing impulse control, tempering your anger, thinking before you speak, making healthy and thoughtful decisions, keeping secrets, containing your thoughts, or communicating more easily, concisely, or clearly. Draw a circle around your target goal. Place the gray candle on top of the paper and light it. Finish by placing the Chariot card just in front of the candle. Let the candle burn out naturally and throw the remnants of cooled wax in the trash.

Why did I choose a gray candle? Gray holds an interesting duality in magick, representing both neutrality and power. In this spell, neutral energies work in tandem with the energies of the Chariot (see below) to create boundaries within the psyche of the practitioner as well as on the astral plane.

Why did I choose the Chariot card? A large portion of the power behind this spell is found within the Hebrew letter *Chet*, which is assigned to this card. Chet means "fence" and is one of the Chariot's hidden meanings. The circle drawn around the target goal in this spell represents a fence. If you imagine the Chariot card as a door or portal, opening it can reveal and invite spirits or energies conducive to creating this fence and lending victory to that which it encloses. The spell acts as a key to this door. The words that you are enclosing within the circle are separated in your subconscious and automatically labeled as "important."

# CHOMPING AT THE BIT

This spell is used to curb impatience, control unwise spending habits, and fight addictions. *Please note:* There are no spells in this book that replace the help and guidance of a medical doctor and/or prescription medication. If you are suffering from the disease of addiction, please seek the help or guidance of a medical professional.

*What you need:*
The Devil card and the Death card from a tarot deck, a black candle (taper or votive), a piece of tumbled crackle quartz, and a medium-sized piece of black tourmaline.

*Instructions:*
Place the Devil card in the middle and center of your altar. Place the Death card on top of the Devil card at a 90° angle, creating an equal-armed cross. Put the piece of crackle quartz and black tourmaline on top of the Death card in the center. Place the black candle above both cards, centered on the Devil card, then light it.

From your heart, ask the energies and spirits that preside over the Death card to remove your burden with harm to none and for the greatest good of all (see sample prayer below). Let the candle burn out naturally and throw the remnants of cooled wax in the trash. Leave all other items for this spell on your altar for a phase of the moon or for fourteen days. After the fourteen-day cycle, return both cards to their tarot deck. You can either leave the crystals on your altar, carry them with you, or place them somewhere that holds meaning to you.

**Sample prayer:**

> *Spirit that presides over the Death card, please release me from the burden of [addiction/anxiety/impatience, etc.] that holds me prisoner. I open my heart to endings and to change. I open my heart to new beginnings. I understand that being hard on myself will only make the healing more difficult, so it is into your hands that I surrender my control and burdens. Let them be transformed into good energy and sent out to the universe with harm to none and for the greatest good of all. So mote it be. Thank you in advance.*

Why did I choose a black candle? The color black represents that which is negative or that which needs to be removed. In this spell, it represents your burden. As the candle burns away, your burden lessens.

Why did I choose the Devil and Death cards? The Devil card represents greed, addiction, and that which holds you prisoner. To understand this card is to understand that which has been repressed and suppressed out of fear. Paradoxically, it also represents a blessing by offering you a lesson to learn or a challenge to overcome. In this way, it acts as a dark angel. In this spell, it represents your burden and is "crossed," or neutralized, by the Death card, which represents just that—the death of something, endings. Its meaning automatically creates new beginnings and new chances. In this spell, it is used to bring death, or an ending, to your burden(s).

Why did I choose crackle quartz and black tourmaline? Crackle quartz is used to ward off evil and to quicken or cleanse the chakras. Black tourmaline is used to remove negativity and to ground the body and mind, especially during difficult times. In this spell, their combination removes burdens and keeps them away, and helps you to regain balance.

# A DARK HORSE

This spell is used to win at games of chance and make money where none is to be found. If you're a gambler, if you like games of chance, or if you like to play lotto, this spell is for you.

**What you need:**
Four pieces of tumbled green aventurine, the nine of clubs from a deck of regular playing cards, and a bowl of your liking large enough to hold the card and the aventurine.

**Instructions:**
After you have assembled all the items needed for this spell, slowly place them on your altar (no particular arrangement is required). Sit quietly in front of your altar, surveying all that you have assembled. When you feel ready, pick up the nine of clubs and say to yourself:

*Bring me good luck as quickly as possible.*

Thank the card and put it in the bowl. Next, pick up all four pieces of aventurine and hold them in your dominant hand as you affirm to yourself:

*Now, I channel all of your positive energies.*

Thank the stones and put them in the bowl with the nine of clubs. Then place the bowl, with all your magickal items in it, in the middle and center of your altar as you say to yourself:

*Bring me money where there is none to be found; let me see the dark horse that will win. Thank you in advance.*

Let your "abundance bowl" stay on your altar for at least nine days and nights. Repeat on the new moon and full moon or as often as you like.

Why did I choose four pieces of green aventurine? In the Practical Qabalah, the number four can be considered a power number. It is associated with a strong foundation, Jupiter (the god of expansion and good luck), his ancient Greek counterpart, Zeus (god of the gods), and with receiving, mercy, and benevolence. It is also associated with the tarot card the Emperor, Major Arcana IV, which embodies power, the astrological force of Aries, decisiveness, authority, strength, and staying power. The number four proves itself worthy of holding energies of strength, power, and, most important, the potential to make great wealth.

Why did I choose green aventurine? Green aventurine is associated with good luck and enhancing and attracting wealth. Its spiritual vibrations can work with the heart chakra. It is here that universal and unconditional love can be found working together to attract abundance and success without creating a karmic disturbance.

Why did I choose the nine of clubs? This card, when used in divinatory work or to read fortunes, is associated with good luck, savings, abundance, and benevolence.

Why did I choose a bowl? A bowl, as a receptacle, represents that aspect of the Creator that manifests itself in the human psyche and within the universe as female, otherwise known as the Goddess or Divine Feminine. In this way, it becomes a symbol of the womb and gestation. It is a symbol of that which gives shape to life.

### ADDITIONAL RESOURCES

Leo, Lawren. *Dragonflame: Tap into Your Reservoir of Power Using Talismans, Manifestation, and Visualization* (Pompton Plains, NJ: New Page Books, 2014).

*Chapter 23*

# EQUINE DREAMS

Through study, meditation, research, and experience, I have assembled a dictionary of terms that can help you interpret your dreams in which horses play a role. Freudian, Jungian, traditional, and esoteric psychology shape the interpretations given here, which are seasoned with elements from folklore and a dash of superstition. I have also drawn heavily on my own psychic experiences and dreams involving horses to compile this reference.

For Sigmund Freud, to dream of riding a horse simply represented sexual intercourse, and this has come to dominate traditional psychology, where dreams of horses are thought to reveal repressed sexual feelings. C. G. Jung felt the horse was a positive sign closely related to the mother archetype, one related to primal drives and inner courage. A complex and multifaceted psychology geared toward finding occult and spiritual symbolism in dreams holds that dreaming of horses may mean sexual liberation, freedom in general, or something incredibly mysterious and cryptic.

Folklore and superstition from different cultures teach us that not every dream of a horse holds the same meaning. The Romans are a good example. They believed the horse was a fertility symbol, but they also saw it—as did many other cultures—as the manifestation of a messenger or guide from the spirit world, like a psychopomp, a being that led the spirits of the dead into the afterlife. In the all-important area of agricultural life, the Romans purportedly hung horse tails in sacred places with great reverence during the winter to ensure a bountiful spring.

To be gifted with an equine message is an honor and holds deep importance. Horses, revered and feared throughout history, are integral to world cultures in art and religion, from the marble horses on the ancient Greek Parthenon to drawings of horses on many of the tarot cards, including Major Arcana XIII (Death, in most traditional tarot decks). Horses permeate myths and sacred texts. Equine imagery surrounds us, and our subconscious is continuously recording our experiences with horses, from birth to death.

As humans, we innately search for meaning in life, constantly seeking answers from outside ourselves. But true meaning comes from inside us—specifically, in the form of dreams. In our dreams, therefore, horses are speaking to us. They are trying to tell us something about ourselves and the world we live in. We watch them in shows on TV and see them at the races and in contests. We take care of them and ride them for competition and enjoyment. As pets, they become our companions. On farms, they are trusted aids. Both graceful and fierce, they have inspired sculptors, painters, and poets for millennia. On a physical level, they bring emotional and mental solace through their contact and gentle interaction with humans, especially those with special needs.

In our dreams, the power the horse holds over us is magnified. In dreams, horses communicate with our core psyche—the part of us that is open to suggestion; the part that can be swayed by inner voices and images, perhaps persuading us to take a different path from the one we were sure was correct for the future. For example, the night before traveling, you may dream of a black horse. A black horse can be frightening and mean death. You awake drenched in sweat, filled with dread, and cancel your flight. And what if you dream of a white horse—an omen of peace and prosperity? If you are experiencing financial woes, this may offer a light at the end of the tunnel.

An equine dream creates a lasting connection to nature, Mother Earth, and our primal instincts. But dreams have many layers, and we must interpret them with care. To dream of a lone horse cantering through a field of lush, green grass can mean what it most immediately evokes: freedom and a complete surrender to passion. But it can also be a sign that a spirit guide is contacting you, a shamanic omen. In this case, it can be a deeply significant emblem of personal empowerment. To determine which of these it may be, you must make yourself aware of your dreams and heed their meanings. If a horse comes to you in a dream, consider it an honor. For it does so of its own free will.

It takes some effort to make the best use of this dictionary. I strongly suggest writing your dreams down in a journal and reading them over to analyze them. Make it a habit to sleep with a pen and paper, in any form, next to you. As soon as you awaken from a dream, jot down everything you can remember. Write as many details as possible:

- Where did the dream take place?

- Was it day? Night? Early morning? Sunset?

- Who was in the dream? Only you? Family? Lover(s)? Friends? Strangers? Aliens?

- What and how did you feel in the dream? Were you angry? Sad? Lonely? Happy? Did you feel delight? Passion? Did your dream body hurt? Were you in pain or limping? Were you in total health? Could you fly?

- What were you thinking, if anything? Was your mind confused or clear? Were you trying to focus on one or multiple images or topics?

Once you are wide awake, go back to your journal entry and fill in the blanks. Write an analysis of each person and thing in your dream, imagining that they are all clear to you, even though they may be a secret reflection of some hidden aspect of yourself.

Then, summarize what you think your dream means. End by recording the day, month, and year of the dream.

The more you journal, the more you tell your subconscious mind that you honor its messages. In turn, you will have more detailed, more significant dreams. Some dreams may even be lucid or prophetic.

Here are a couple tips. My mentor once told me that, to interpret a dream correctly, you should use only one dream-interpretation book, because, if you use too many, you can confuse your psyche. Choose one you like and trust it! This is an act of empowerment. You are bringing this book into your magickal sphere. In return, it will automatically align with your psyche, your subconscious, and your personal dreamscape.

# SPELL TO CALL YOUR
# PERSONAL DREAM HORSE

You can also bring a personal dream horse into your magickal sphere. It can be any breed, shape, size, or color. It can even have wings or a unicorn's horn. Give it a golden tail, a lilac mane, fiery eyes—whatever you like. This horse is destined to become a part of your secret magickal mind. It can bring you solace, reveal the future, open doors to occult information, or simply help you escape your everyday life and take you on a midnight dream ride. Determine what your dream horse looks like, give it a name, and, before you go to bed, tell it what you want by writing a wish on a piece of paper. Put the paper under your pillow, and chant this spell three times:

> *Come to me, oh dream horse mine,*
>
> *Through the veil where there's no time!*
>
> *Carry me now throughout the night;*

*Be my ride and give me sight.*

*Watch over me, talk to me, clearly and true;*

*Forever come fast when I call on you.*

Sweet dreams,

Lawren Leo

# EQUINE DREAM DICTIONARY

***apple:*** To dream of an apple connotes that knowledge concerning love and the occult will soon enter your life. To dream of eating an apple means you will have an epiphany concerning love, writing, and the occult. To dream of a horse or horses eating apples means that your love spell will work soon. It also means that a lover will enter your life soon.

***barn:*** To dream of a barn connotes good luck and success.

***barn fire:*** To dream of a barn on fire or collapsing is a sign of bankruptcy and financial failure.

***bit:*** To dream of a bit means fear of failure. You are doing something to hold yourself back from realizing your fullest potential. Stop accepting a role where you always take second place.

***blacksmith:*** A dream about a blacksmith connotes that a hidden strength will be awakened that will allow you to accomplish a difficult task successfully. It also means that you possess a special understanding of horses. It can also symbolize inner strength, good luck, prosperity, and connection with Mother Earth and nature.

***blinkers:*** A dream about blinkers connotes narrow-mindedness and a sheltered life.

***boots, cowboy:*** To dream of cowboy boots connotes a connection to nature. They are an omen of adventure entering your life. If they have spurs, the adventure will not be pleasant, but will result in good fortune. If they don't, the adventure will be pleasant and will result in wisdom gained from experience.

*boots, English riding (leather, knee-high):* To dream of wearing leather riding boots connotes that good luck in a long-term, successful love relationship is coming your way. To see leather riding boots connotes wisdom in a difficult situation.

*bow string:* To dream of a bow strung with hair from a horse's tail connotes an end to problems and better communication. It also means that beauty and harmony are around the corner.

*breed and/or registry papers:* These papers connote news of an adoption or news of a long-lost relative.

*calf-roping:* To dream of watching calf-roping means that you feel helpless and vulnerable. To dream that you are roping calves means that you are taking away someone's innocence or taking advantage of someone in a vulnerable situation.

*carrot:* To dream of a carrot connotes that a new business venture will present itself soon, and that it will be too good to be true. To eat a carrot connotes health. To dream of a horse or horses eating carrots means that you will have digestive problems.

*centaur, female (centaurides):* To dream of a female centaur connotes that you will look more youthful and that your physical appearance will grow more beautiful. If you dream of two or more, beware gossip among women.

*centaur, male:* To dream of a male centaur connotes that you must beware of an impending sexual assault. It also means that a romantic situation may turn physically abusive.

*centaur, young:* To dream of a young centaur connotes a capricious heart.

*chaps:* A dream about chaps connotes emotional resilience. It also means a time of celibacy. On the darker side, it means a temporary state of inceldom ("incel"—a person unable to find a romantic or sexual partner despite desiring one).

*chariot:* A dream about driving a chariot connotes taking control of your destiny. If you dream of seeing someone in a chariot, your destiny is being blocked by another. If you dream of an empty chariot, it is an omen of wasting time.

*coach, carriage:* A dream about a coach or carriage means you will soon receive a marriage proposal or have good fortune in your love life.

*colt (young male horse):* A dream about a young male horse connotes playfulness. It also means physical brawls. (See *filly* for young female horse.)

*corn:* To dream of corn growing healthy in a field means wealth. In general, corn is auspicious. To dream of a horse eating corn, or feeding corn to a horse, means that you will become prosperous. To dream of rotting or unhealthy corn means a loss in finances.

*cowboy, gaucho:* To dream of a cowboy or gaucho, or to dream of being a cowboy or gaucho, means you are in the process of stopping romantic feelings that are getting out of control. It connotes regaining control over your life in general. It also means a desire to be alone in order to regain control over your life and emotions.

*crop:* A dream about a crop connotes a fiery form of discipline that you are using on others. You are a victim of or are using sexual manipulation. It can also connote an increase in willpower and a short respite from laziness. If you are disciplined with a crop you will suffer humiliation and insult.

*currycomb:* A dream about this type of comb, used for grooming when the horse is particularly dirty or shedding, may mean that you are surrounded by annoying people and events that are very difficult to remove from your life.

*donkey:* To dream of riding a donkey connotes a difficult journey ahead. To dream of a donkey itself connotes stubbornness and a need for humility.

*equestrian vaulting/dancing:* To dream about equestrian dancing or vaulting connotes successfully accomplishing a seemingly impossible task.

*falconry:* To practice falconry on horseback connotes power, knowledge, superior ideas. It can also mean an auspicious dream.

*farrier:* See **blacksmith**.

*feedbag:* To dream of the leather or canvas bag attached over a horse's muzzle for feeding can have several meanings. An empty feedbag connotes sickness and a loss of money. A feedbag full of grain connotes good luck and temporarily appeasing business matters and business partners.

*fence:* To dream of a fence connotes a barrier. If you find the gate and pass through, you will find success. To jump over a fence means that you will find a way over barriers and obstacles in a sly manner. If it is a fence that you have put up, it means that you have strong boundaries and protection. To dream of horses enclosed behind a fence means your sexual energies are being kept under control for later use. To dream of horses or a horse escaping a fenced-in area or jumping over a fence means that your sexual energies are out of control, but that you will find a creative outlet that will help you succeed. See also **horse, stumbling over a jump** and **show jumping**.

*filly (young female horse):* To dream about a young female horse connotes playfulness. It also means gossip. (See **colt** for young male horse.)

*fine harness horse:* To watch fine harness horses connotes buying new, elegant clothing. It also means an increase in mature conversations. To drive a fine harness horse connotes new friends in high places and an increase in confidence and prosperity. To remove the harness connotes that time for reflection is needed to assess the situation further.

*foal (horse of either sex, less than one year old):* To dream of a foal connotes playfulness and unexplored abilities. It also means shirking responsibilities and, in certain situations, can represent codependence.

*foxhunting:* To dream you are in a fox hunt connotes that you must beware of deceit from a person close to you. To dream of a fox being killed is an omen of ill fortune.

*gelding:* Aside from feelings of emasculation in general, a dream about a gelding specifically represents rejection by a potential romantic partner—unrequited love.

*glue:* To dream of a horse glue factory connotes that dreadful news will soon be revealed. To dream of glue connotes the feeling of inadequacy to make relationships stick.

*grain:* (See **millet**.)

*grass:* To dream of green grass connotes wealth and vitality. If it needs to be mowed or if you are mowing it, you will reorganize the business and financial aspects of your life soon. If a horse or horses are eating grass and there is an abundance of it, you will experience fulfillment in your life. If a horse or horses are eating grass and there is not an abundance of it, you will experience hardships in life.

*halter:* A dream about a halter may mean that your spirit guide wants to lead you.

*hay:* To dream of burning hay connotes bad luck. (See **timothy grass or hay**.)

*helmet, riding:* A dream about a riding helmet can connote protection from what you believe is vulnerable. Also, protection from mental illnesses and anxiety.

*hoof:* To dream of a horse's hoof or hooves connotes insight, wealth, and pleasant messages. If the hoof or hooves are unhealthy, it means the opposite.

**hops:** To dream of hops connotes finding the core issue of health problems, both physical and emotional. To dream of drinking hops—via beer, tincture, or tea—means you will learn how to heal yourself naturally without traditional medication. To dream of a horse or horses eating hops connotes extra vitality and stability.

**horse:** A dream about a horse means freedom, strength, vitality, and a surge in psychic abilities.

**horse (asleep standing):** A dream about a sleeping horse standing up connotes an important issue is being ignored. If the horse is lying on its side sleeping, this increases the importance of the issue.

**horse (attacking, biting, chasing):** To dream that a horse is chasing or trying to attack you connotes suppressed emotions that are starting to surface. To dream you are being chased by a white horse means you are running away from financial duties and career responsibilities. To dream you are being chased by a black horse means fear of growing old and fear of death. To dream a horse is biting you connotes post-traumatic stress disorder (PTSD) and can also be a warning to question your actions regarding a serious situation.

**horse (battlefield):** To dream of a horse or horses on a battlefield connotes grief and struggle. If you are on a horse in battle, you will soon encounter a lawsuit. It also means that you view life as a never-ending struggle.

**horse (being thrown from):** Falling off or being thrown from a horse connotes discomfort, both emotional and sometimes physical. (See **horse, white** and **horse, black, bucking**.)

**horse (black):** A black horse represents freedom, perhaps even freedom from the earthly plane. A dream about a black horse is an omen of illness or death. If you dream you are riding a black horse that is walking, it is a warning to watch your spiritual, mental, emotional, and/or physical health. If you dream you are riding a black stallion that is walking, you have control over your sex drive. If the horse is trotting or cantering, you will experience a newly found power. If it is galloping, you are sure to be handed a life-changing opportunity.

*horse (black, bucking):* If you dream you are riding a black horse that is bucking and don't fall off, it means that you will fall ill, but eventually recuperate. If you fall, the illness will be severe.

*horse (bolting):* A bolting horse connotes a loss of impulse control. If you dream you are on a horse and it bolts, it means you are allowing yourself to be carried away by your passions and impulses. There may be difficulties in your near future.

*horse (castration):* To dream of a horse being castrated connotes an enemy gaining power over you. It also means a loss of power and repressed feelings, and is an overall ill portent.

*horse (circus):* To dream of a horse in a circus means you are surrounded by two-faced individuals and gossip.

*horse (cooling down):* A dream about a horse cooling down is a signal to slow down, stop worrying, and take care of yourself. It also means preparing for retirement or the need to prepare for retirement. It connotes a time of repose after hard work.

*horse (cribbing):* To dream of a horse cribbing ("crib biting") connotes sexual frustration, anxiety, and obsessive-compulsive behavior. It can also be a warning that you are about to choose a romantic partner out of desperation.

*horse (dead):* This is a sure sign of illness, especially emotional. If you see flies on the horse, it represents mental anguish.

*horse (eye):* A horse's eye can be an omen that someone is stalking you and accessing intimate portions of your life, especially via social media. It also represents a cheating lover.

*horse (feral):* A feral horse is the descendant of domesticated horses, whereas a wild horse comes from a lineage that has never been domesticated. To dream of a single feral horse running free connotes issues with impulse control. It also means you will soon have an epiphany. To dream of a herd of feral horses connotes an encounter, either pleasant or unpleasant, with your wild or darker side. It also means you will have an unexpected epiphany related to your sexual orientation.

*horse (fighting):* To dream of two horses fighting connotes confusion with sexual identity. If you fight with the horse, it means you are thinking of committing a crime that will lead to misfortune.

*horse (foaling/giving birth):* To dream of a horse giving birth connotes uplifting others with a positive attitude. It also means inner confidence and productive endeavors.

*horse (gray):* A gray horse connotes obstacles.

*horse (in a petting zoo):* A dream about a horse in a petting zoo connotes emotional security and comfort. If you are not petting the horses/ponies and are a bystander, it can indicate feelings of inadequacy stemming from childhood abuse or from being bullied.

*horse (in a stall):* To dream of a horse in a stall connotes an increase in willpower and self-discipline.

*horse (in armor):* A dream about a horse in armor connotes low self-esteem, especially centered around feelings of sexual inadequacy. It is an ill portent.

*horse (lame):* A lame horse can indicate a change of career, not necessarily for the better. It also connotes loneliness. Riding a lame, wounded, or limping horse foretells an unfortunate encounter with a lawyer, police, or law enforcement.

*horse (lying down):* To dream of a horse lying down connotes a short respite from burdens and a short standstill in your sex life.

*horse (manure, feces):* To dream of horse manure is always auspicious. To smell or touch horse manure also connotes good fortune and money.

*horse (mating):* To dream of two horses mating connotes a strong or renewed sex drive.

*horse (mounting):* To dream of mounting a horse with confidence means you will soon advance at work. To dream of another mounting your horse against your will connotes conjugal infidelity.

*horse (nipple):* A horse's nipple can connote stability, peace, and contentment. It also means news of a pregnancy.

*horse (passing gas):* To dream about a horse passing gas connotes release of evil and negativity.

*horse (penis):* To dream of a horse with a large penis connotes gaining stature. To dream of a small penis means the opposite. To dream of touching a horse's penis connotes a lack of affection. To dream of a misshapen penis connotes someone coming into your life as a lover, but under false pretenses (usually for money or to obtain a higher social status). To dream of a penis that is branching or growing more than one tip connotes fertility and having children. It could also mean pregnancy and foals of horses you own or know.

*horse (performing dressage):* To dream of a horse performing dressage or riding a horse and performing dressage connotes refining skills. To dream of winning a dressage competition connotes refining skills enough to surpass all obstacles and to achieve great success.

*horse (plowing):* To dream about a horse with a plow connotes help in business matters after a time of hard work. It can also mean luck in sales and that recognition will come after hard work.

*horse (rearing):* A rearing horse connotes anxiety and health issues connected with the central nervous system.

*horse (red or sorrel):* A red or sorrel horse connotes receiving awards.

*horse (riding):* Riding a horse in a dream can mean a release from burdens.

**horse (rolling over on you):** To dream of a horse rolling over on you while riding it connotes a financial and romantic loss. If you remount successfully, it connotes you will recover and be even better than before.

**horse (rubbing against a fence):** To dream of a horse rubbing against a fence, or to dream of a horse rubbing its mane or tail against a fence, connotes discomfort, anxiety, or illness.

**horse (running toward you):** A dream about a horse running toward you connotes a person or people coming to you for advice.

**horse (running wild in an open field):** A dream about a horse running wild in an open field connotes that all obstacles that are preventing you from obtaining a special goal, especially one connected with freedom, will be removed.

**horse (semen):** To dream of horse semen connotes money and lust. The more semen, the more money and the stronger the feeling of lust.

**horse (shape-shifting):** A dream about a shape-shifting horse is a gift from Horse Spirit indicating the success of your spellwork.

**horse (shod):** To see a shod horse, to shoe a horse, or to see one being shod connotes obstacles and bad luck.

**horse (shooting):** To shoot a horse means that you will soon end a relationship.

**horse (slaughtered):** To dream of killing a horse or seeing a horse slaughtered in a dream is an ill omen and means financial problems. It can also mean that you are suffering from post-traumatic stress disorder.

**horse (spooked or shying):** To dream of riding a horse that is frightened or spooked means that you will need to make a sudden move in your living situation. If you are leading a horse and it shies, or if you see a horse shy, you or your lover will change your mind about maintaining loyalties. It can also mean a shift in consciousness, or a change of personal philosophy.

*horse (stepping on you):* To dream of being accidentally stepped on by a horse connotes a broken heart. To dream that a horse accidentally steps on your toe and breaks it connotes a delay in plans, especially finance and love.

*horse (stumbling over a jump):* To dream of a horse stumbling over a jump connotes financial loss and that a long-awaited project will be jeopardized. (See *show jumping* and *fence*.)

*horse (swimming):* To dream of a horse swimming connotes anxiety and problems with the law. To dream of swimming with a horse or riding a horse through water connotes pleasure and ecstasy.

*horse (teeth):* To dream of a horse's tooth or teeth connotes the foretelling of your death or news of a death or loss.

*horse (tomb of):* A dream about a horse's tomb connotes that you are about to venture into parts of your sexuality that you have kept buried.

*horse (urine):* To dream of a horse urinating on you connotes joy and pleasure. To watch a horse urinate connotes a release of sexual repression.

*horse (vagina):* If you are a female and dream of a horse's vagina it means that you will or would like to use your sexuality/sex to get ahead and for power over others. If you are a male and dream of a horse's vagina it means that you try to avoid sex out of fear of low self-esteem. To dream of touching a horse's vagina connotes sexual needs unfulfilled.

*horse (white):* White horses indicate that an increase in love, finances, and/or career is in sight. If you dream of a white horse in a snowy landscape, however, spiritual help is on the way. If you dream you are riding a white horse, you will hear news of a marriage or engagement, or will be married or engaged in the near future. It also means stability in love, health, finances, or career. Riding a white horse that is bucking and not falling off means that you will successfully face known and unknown troubles, but only after a brief spate of anxiety. If you fall, the troubles will become more severe and may turn into losses.

*horse (winning a competition):* A horse winning a competition connotes recognition and fulfillment of desires, or abundance and prosperity. It also means emotional restoration and self-confidence.

*horse auction:* To dream of bidding at a horse auction connotes having a hard time moving ahead and feeling as if you should give up on your sex life. It also means problems and confusion with people in general.

*horse racing (Ban'ei):* To dream of watching Ban'ei racing (a type of Japanese horse racing in which draft horses pull heavy sleds) means that there are many burdened, hardworking people around you. To dream of being in a Ban'ei race means that your courage and will to live will be tested to their breaking point, but not without reward.

*horse racing (Thoroughbred):* To dream of watching a horse race connotes a strong sense of competition in your immediate trajectory for success, love, or improvement in any aspect of life. To dream of being in a horse race connotes being at the center of competition in work or love, and strong ambition. It can also mean fighting for your health.

*horseball:* To dream of watching horseball connotes good news from financial institutions and important groups of men. To dream you are playing horseball successfully connotes good luck with stocks, cryptocurrency, and foreign markets. To dream you are playing horseball unsuccessfully connotes competition, loss of finances, and losing your spouse or romantic partner to a man, not a woman.

*horsefly:* To dream of a horsefly connotes mental anguish over one particular problem.

**horseshoe:** A dream about a horseshoe can mean it is a good time to gamble. If the ends are up, it represents good luck. But if the ends point down, it represents bad luck. It can also connote protection from thievery because of the magickal, apotropaic properties of iron.

**horseshoes (the game):** Dreaming about the game of horseshoes can mean a setback in business and career if you lose, a windfall in business and career if you win. If you are watching the game, you desire success in business, but it is presently out of reach.

**jousting:** Jousting connotes a battle of the wills, especially in a romantic and sexual relationship. It also means trying to win over the heart of a man or woman.

**knight:** If you are a woman and you dream of a white knight, it is a portent of good news involving a long-awaited love. If you are a gay or pansexual man, it holds the same meaning. If you are a heterosexual man, it means you are challenging yourself to be a hero and more courageous in matters of love. If you dream of a black knight, it holds the reverse for all meanings of the white knight. Seeing a knight in armor connotes travel and adventure. If you are wearing armor, it connotes temporary protection from financial and health problems.

**mailman:** To dream of a mailman delivering mail on horseback means that you will soon hear news from a loved one. To speak with a mailman delivering mail on horseback means that you will be the one to reach out to a loved one.

**mane:** A dream of a horse's mane can indicate a fear of growing old. It also connotes reminiscence over childhood phases in your life. To dream of trimming a mane connotes separation, divorce, and abandonment.

**mane (braided):** To dream of a braided mane prepared for show connotes success in modeling, acting, speaking in front of a crowd, or any public presentation or career.

**mane (roaching or hogging):** To dream of shaving or roaching a mane connotes obstacles removed that have been preventing success and popularity.

**mare:** A dream about a mare means that your feminine side is ready to be nurtured at a controlled pace. It indicates creativity and gentle force.

**mare (pregnant):** A dream about a pregnant mare means that your feminine side is ready to present creativity and new ideas. It also connotes meeting new friends.

**mare (with foal or foals):** To dream of a mare with her foal/foals connotes strong protection from the mother goddess and protection from enemies, especially neighbors that may wish you ill.

**mare's milk:** Mare's milk connotes sustenance, wealth, and good luck. If it is sour, it can mean bad luck, illness, and bad news. To dream of drinking mare's milk connotes victory in any battle. To dream of milking a mare connotes that problems with digestion and bones will improve. To serve mare's milk means that you will be volunteering for a good cause. To see a friend drink mare's milk means that person will be your ally and help you overcome an enemy or enemies. To see an enemy drink mare's milk means defeat in any battle.

**meadow:** To dream of a beautiful, open meadow connotes that all obstacles are removed and protracted moments of peace. To dream of a dried-up meadow connotes depression about your current state of affairs, with no prospect of enjoyment in the near future. It is an omen that it is time for you to move on from a stale or stagnant career and/or relationship.

**millet:** To dream of scattering millet to feed farm stock connotes that extra effort will be needed in business and in love. To dream of millet shells connotes bad luck and sadness concerning children, especially daughters. To dream of growing millet connotes an increase in love, health, and wealth.

*molasses:* To dream of molasses connotes confusion with love. To dream of eating molasses or being served molasses means that you will soon make a decision regarding love. It also means generosity from next-door neighbors.

*mule:* To dream of riding a mule connotes safe travels. To dream of a mule itself connotes good news from afar.

*neigh:* In dreams, neighing warns of imminent danger.

*oats:* To dream of eating oats means you will have a full recovery soon. It also connotes happiness and health. To dream of feeding oats to another person means that you will play an important part in the recuperation process of someone close to you—someone whose feelings toward you may not be reciprocated. To dream of feeding oats to a horse or horses means that you will bond with your horse or a new horse. It also means that you will derive pleasure from Mother Earth and being in nature.

*paddock:* To dream of a horse paddock connotes letting go of something lesser in order to achieve something greater, for it is a sacrifice to give up a part of the pasture to make a proper paddock. It also means you will soon receive a gift of money.

*Pegasus:* Pegasus is symbolic of inspiration and wisdom. A dream about him may mean that an important decision will present itself shortly, or that you will resolve a question to which you already have the answer.

*polo:* To dream of watching a polo match connotes rubbing elbows with the rich and famous. To dream of being in a polo match connotes long-distance travel, foreigners, and success in new endeavors.

*racetrack:* To dream about a racetrack connotes that you view life as a competition and are entering a time of stress. Look into stress management in order to move forward and win at the game of life.

*reins:* A dream that involves reins means that you are taking charge of your destiny by becoming a co-creator with the universe. It also connotes spiritual awareness and enlightenment. It can also show that increased responsibilities will lead to success.

*riding (bareback):* To dream of riding a white horse bareback connotes success in love, health, or career after a struggle. To dream of riding a black horse bareback connotes a long recuperation from a broken heart or from a mental, emotional, or physical illness. (see *horse, white* and *horse, black*).

*riding (naked):* Riding naked connotes the necessity to confront your sexual desires honestly, especially about a specific person.

*riding (side-saddle):* Riding side-saddle connotes that old fashioned values are interfering with your love life.

*riding (trail):* To dream of riding a horse solo or with a group on a trail ride connotes recuperation from illness, relaxation, and that you will soon develop a deeper connection to Mother Earth and nature. It also connotes continued success in business, especially the retail industry.

*riding arena or ring:* To see a riding arena (schooling ring for horse riding) in a dream or to be in a riding arena in a dream can connote an increase in self-discipline and a big change or move coming into your life.

*rocking horse (curved rockers or iron straps):* To see a rocking horse in a dream means you are confronting suppressed feelings of sexuality. It also means sexual frustration and the need to be comforted. To dream of riding a rocking horse connotes embracing your sexuality and self-comfort. It also means your insomnia will soon be healed, perhaps through prescribed medication. In addition, it can indicate winning at the races, especially horse races, but not without an emotional price.

*rodeo:* To dream of watching a rodeo means that people around you (business partners, family, friends) are beginning to take control of their lives. To dream that you are in a rodeo means that you will begin taking control of your life and experience fewer difficulties.

*saddle:* A saddle is an omen that your life will improve shortly. To dream of a saddle connotes taking back control over a situation. To dream you are lifting, carrying, or putting a saddle on a horse means that you are "saddled" with burdens.

*saddle (English):* To dream of an English saddle means you will successfully start a new business. To dream of riding a horse with an English saddle means that you will start a new adventure soon. It also means to be cautious of judgmental people.

*saddle (Western):* To dream of a Western saddle means that you will shortly embark on a long-term goal. To dream of riding a horse with a Western saddle means that you will successfully reach your goal after building it slowly and confidently.

*Sagittarius (constellation):* To dream of the astrological sign of Sagittarius connotes that adventure and affection will soon be entering your life. If you are an equestrian, you will soon change horse instructors. It also means that someone will soon give you valuable advice.

*salt lick:* A salt lick connotes that you will soon receive or give wise advice. To dream of a horse at a salt lick is an omen of ill-health. It also means your system is lacking necessary minerals. To dream you are tasting or licking the salt is an omen of good health and that your wish will soon be granted.

*Samurai riding a horse:* To dream that you are a Samurai riding a horse means that you will successfully strategize a difficult task or project. It also connotes loyalty, usually in business or partnership, but also romantically.

*seahorse:* Seahorses connote that a new love will soon be entering your life. They also mean that you will meet someone with whom you will have a deep and profound emotional connection. Beware loneliness.

**show hunter:** To dream of watching show-hunter horses connotes strategic thinking. To dream that you are showing a horse connotes that you are in a situation that demands further analysis and strategy before acting.

**show jumping:** Show jumping connotes the proper use of power and discernment. It can also mean using your wisdom to understand when people are abusing their power. To dream of successfully going over a jump connotes that abundance will quickly manifest in your life. (See **horse, stumbling over a jump** and **fence.**)

**snicker:** A horse snickering connotes getting in touch with that part of you that wants to give you confidence, strength, and power.

**snort:** A horse snorting connotes getting in touch with that part of you that wants to give you an important message concerning friendship, travel, love, or business.

**spurs:** A dream involving spurs connotes ambition, cruelty, and motivation.

**stables:** Stables represent sexual repression and suppression. They can also connote contained libido and the beginning of a sexual awakening.

**stallion:** See **horse, black.**

**stirrup:** Stirrups indicate that you will be offered help in your career. They can also connote motivation.

**tack room:** To dream that you are in a tack room or a dream of horse tack itself connotes a desire for control over impulses.

**tail (braided for show):** To dream of a braided tail prepared for show means that you will do well on upcoming scholastic tests.

**tail (docked):** To dream of a tail cut short, right below the natural dock, so as not to be caught in the trappings of the harness when driving (not to be confused with the inhumane practice of cutting the muscle of the dock for esthetic effect), means obstacles will be removed that have been preventing you from success in farming, real estate, agriculture, and gardening.

*tail (free flowing):* A horse with a free-flowing tail indicates protection, good luck—especially in romance and physical health—and marriage. To trim a tail connotes abandonment by friends. It also means military embarrassment. (See *mane.*)

*timothy (grass or hay):* To dream of timothy grass or hay connotes success in business and money. To dream of horses eating timothy hay or grass connotes that investments will pay off in time.

*trough:* To dream of a trough filled with fodder or water connotes that wealth is close at hand. To dream of a white horse, or a horse of any color other than black, eating or drinking from a trough means wealth is at hand and that you will be victorious over enemies. To dream of a black horse eating or drinking from a trough means a loss in finances and that your enemies are conspiring behind your back.

*twitch:* If you are using a twitch—most often a rope or leather cord used to clamp the horse's upper lip as an aid in handling and disciplining—it is a sure sign that you are afraid of your sexuality. If you see someone using a twitch, it is a sign that you are grappling with issues of social injustice, racism, and sexism.

*unicorn:* To dream of a unicorn connotes overall health, successful medical treatment(s), and successful surgeries. If the unicorn comes to you, it is a sure sign of fame and success. If you dream you are riding a unicorn, you will soon enter a long-term, successful love relationship.

*whinny:* Whinnying connotes getting in touch with that part of you that wants to give a warning concerning friendship, travel, love, or business.

*winged horse:* To dream of any winged horse connotes kundalini rising. It also means putting your sexual energy to use in a pragmatic, meaningful way. (See *Pegasus.*)

# ADDITIONAL RESOURCES

*Secondary sources*

Freud, Sigmund. *The Interpretation of Dreams*, trans. A. A. Brill (Digireads.com Publishing, 2017).

Jung, C. G. *The Archetypes and the Collective Unconscious*, trans. R. F. C. Hull, 2nd ed. (Princeton, NJ: Princeton University Press, 1981).

—————. *Dreams*, trans. R. F. C. Hull, rev. ed. (Princeton, NJ: Princeton University Press, 2010).

Rich, Janet Bubar. *Riding on Horses' Wings: Reimagining Today's Horse for Tomorrow's World* (New York: Peter Lang Publishing, Inc., 2016).

# BIBLIOGRAPHY

## Primary Sources

Apuleius. *The Golden Ass*, trans. Sarah Ruden (New Haven, CT: Yale University Press, 2011).

Byock, Jesse, trans. *The Prose Edda* (London: Penguin Classics, 2005).

Condos, Theony, trans. and comm. *Star Myths of the Greeks and Romans: A Sourcebook* (Grand Rapids, MI: Phanes Press, 1997).

*Dhyana Sloka* (Verse for Meditation) by Vedanta Desika (1268–1370), trans. P. R. Ramachander. Retrieved from *http://celextel.org* (accessed 2/3/2018).

Evelyn-White, Hugh G., trans. *Hesiod, Homeric Hymns, Epic Cycle, Homerica* (London: William Heinemann Ltd., 1914).

Faulkner, Raymond, trans. *The Egyptian Book of the Dead: The Book of Going Forth by Day* (San Francisco: Chronicle Books, 1994).

Gardner, John, and John Maier, trans. *Gilgamesh* (New York: Vintage Books, 1984).

Herodotus. *The Histories*, ed. Paul Cartledge, trans. Tom Holland (New York: Penguin Books, 2015).

Homer. *The Iliad*, trans. Caroline Alexander (London: HarperCollins, 2015).

——————. *The Iliad: A New Prose Translation*, trans. Martin Hammond (London: Penguin Books, 1987).

——————. *The Odyssey*, trans. Walter Shewring (Oxford, England: Oxford University Press, 1980).

Jacobus de Voragine. *The Golden Legend: Readings on the Saints*, trans. William Granger Ryan, vol. 1 (Princeton, NJ: Princeton University Press, 1993).

Kammenhuber, A. *Hippologia hethitica* (Wiesbaden, Germany: Harrassowitz, 1961).

Komjathy, Louis, trans. *Taming the Wild Horse: An Annotated Translation and Study of the Daoist Horse Taming Pictures* (New York: Columbia University Press, 2017).

Lichtheim, Miriam. *Ancient Egyptian Literature*, vol. 2 (Berkeley, CA: University of California Press, 1976).

Menon, Ramash. *Bhagavata Purana: The Holy Book of Vishnu*, 2 vols. (Calcutta, India: Rupa & Co., 2011).

Nonnus, *Dionysiaca*, 3 vols., trans. W. H. D. Rouse (Cambridge, MA: Harvard University Press, 1940).

Ō no Yasumaro, compiler. *The Kojiki (An Account of Ancient Matters)*, trans. Gustav Heldt (New York: Columbia University Press, 2004).

——————. *The Kojiki*, trans. Basil Hall Chamberlain (1919). Retrieved from *https://sacred-texts.com*.

Ovid. *Fasti*, 2nd ed., trans. James G. Frazer, rev. G. P. Goold (Cambridge, MA: Harvard University Press, 1931).

Philostratus the Elder, Philostratus the Younger, and Callistratus. *Philostratus the Elder, Imagines. Philostratus the Younger, Imagines. Callistratus, Descriptions*, trans. Arthur Fairbanks (Cambridge, MA: Harvard University Press, 1931).

Pindar. *Pindar II: Nemean Odes, Isthmian Odes, Fragments*, trans. William H. Race (Cambridge, MA: Harvard University Press, 1997).

Quintus Smyrnaeus. *The Fall of Troy*, trans. A. S. Way (London: William Heinemann, 1913).

Sandars, N. K., trans. *Poems of Heaven and Hell from Ancient Mesopotamia* (London: Penguin Books, 1971).

Saxo Grammaticus. *The First Nine Books of the Danish History of Saxo Grammaticus*, trans. Oliver Elton (London: David Nutt, 1894).

Schiltberger, Johannes. *Hans Schiltbergers Reisebuch nach der Nürnberger Handschrift*, ed. Valentin Langmantel (Tübingen, Germany: Litterarischen Verlein in Stuttgart, 1885).

Smyser, H. M. "Ibn Fadlan's Account of the Rus with Some Commentary and Some Allusions to *Beowulf*." In Jess B. Bessinger, Jr. and Robert P. Creed, ed., *Franciplegius: Medieval and Linguistic Studies in Honor of Francis Peabody Magoun, Jr.* (New York: New York University Press, 1965), pp. 92–119.

Statius. *Statius: Thebaid, Books 8–12. Achilleid*, trans. D. R. Shackleton Bailey (Cambridge, MA: Harvard University Press, 2004).

Tacitus, Cornelius. *Tacitus I, Agricola. Germania. Dialogus*, trans. M. Hutton and W. Peterson, Loeb Classical Library, rev. ed. (Cambridge, MA: Harvard University Press, 1914).

Winterbottom, Michael, and Michael Lapidge, ed. and trans. *The Early Lives of St. Dunstan* (Oxford, England: Oxford University Press, 2012).

Xenophon, *The Works of Xenophon*, trans. H. G. Dakyns, vol. 3, part 2, Three Essays: On the Duties of a Cavalry General, On Horsemanship, and On Hunting (London: Macmillan and Co., 1897). Retrieved from *https://archive.org* (accessed 9/26/2019).

## Secondary Sources

### Websites

*http://aaanativearts.com*
*http://arkive.org*
*http://epona.net*
*http://firstpeople.us*
*http://maakcenter.org*
*https://etymonline.com*

### Paper and Electronic Sources

Afanas'ev, A. N. *Russian Folk-Tales*, trans. Leonard A. Magnus (New York: E. P. Dutton & Company, 1916).

Alvarado, Denise. *The Magic of Marie Laveau: Embracing the Spiritual Legacy of the Voodoo Queen of New Orleans* (Newburyport, MA: Weiser Books, 2019).

Andrews, Ted. *Animal Speak* (Woodbury, MN: Llewellyn Publications, 1993).

Anthony, David W. *The Horse, the Wheel, and Language: How Bronze-Age Riders from the European Steppes Shaped the Modern World* (Princeton, NJ: Princeton University Press, 2010).

Anthony, David W. "Horses, ancient Near East and Pharaonic Egypt." In Roger S. Bagnall, et al., ed., *The Encyclopedia of Ancient History* (Chichester, England: Blackwell Publishing Ltd., 2013), pp. 3311–3314.

Babu, Sridhara D. *Hayagriva: The Horse-Headed Deity in Indian Culture* (Tirupati, India: Sri Venkateswara University, 1990).

Bahn, Paul, and Michel Lorblanchet. *The First Artists: In Search of the World's Oldest Art* (London: Thames and Hudson, 2017).

Barley, Nigel. *Nigerian Arts Revisited* (Paris: Somogy Art Publish-ers, 2016).

Barrett, W. P., trans. *The Trial of Jeanne d'Arc* (New York: Gotham House, Inc., 1932). Retrieved from *https://sourcebooks.fordham.edu* (accessed 10/2/2019).

Beard, Mary, John North, and Simon Price. *Religions of Rome*, vol. 1 (Cambridge, England: Cambridge University Press, 1998).

Beyerl, Paul. *Compendium of Herbal Magic* (Blaine, WA: Phoenix Publishing, 1998).

Boyd, Lee, and Katherine A. Houpt, ed. *Przewalski's Horse: The History and Biology of an Endangered Species* (Albany, NY: State University of New York Press, 1994).

Bramshaw, Vikki. *Dionysos: Exciter to Frenzy. A Study of the God Dionysos: History, Myth, and Lore* (London: Avalonia, 2013).

Bruchac III, Joseph. *Native American Animal Stories* (Golden, CO: Fulcrum Publishing, 1992).

Bullia, Cassandra. *Transcending Borders: An Analysis of Epona Worship Cross-Culturally and Her Roman Adoption*. Retrieved from *https://academia.edu* (accessed 6/6/2018).

Burkert, Walter. *Greek Religion*, trans. John Raffan (Cambridge, MA: Basil Blackwell Publisher and Harvard University Press, 1985).

Bychowski, Gabrielle. "Gender, Sexism, and the Middle Ages, Part 3: Were There Transgender People in the Middle Ages?" *The PublicMedievalist. Com* (November 2018). Retrieved from *https://publicmedievalist.com* (accessed 12/2/2018).

Cavallo, Adolfo Salvatore. *The Unicorn Tapestries at the Metropolitan Museum of Art* (New Haven, CT: Yale University Press, 1998).

Cayce, Edgar. *The Book of the Revelation: A Commentary Based on a Study of Twenty-Three Psychic Discourses by Edgar Cayce* (Virginia Beach, VA: A. R. E. Press, 1969).

Chamberlin, J. Edward. *How the Horse Has Shaped Civilizations* (New York: Bluebridge, 2006).

Clark, La Verne Harrell. *They Sang for Horses: The Impact of the Horse on Navajo and Apache Folklore* (Boulder, CO: Arizona University Press, 2001).

Cole, Herbert M. *Igbo: Visions of Africa Series* (Milan, Italy: 5 Continents Editions, 2013).

——————. *Invention and Tradition: The Art of Southeast Nigeria* (Munich, Germany: Prestel Verlag, 2012).

Collins, Billie Jean, ed. *A History of the Animal World in the Ancient Near East* (Leiden, Netherlands: Brill, 2001).

Condos, Theony. *Star Myths of the Greeks and Romans: A Sourcebook* (Grand Rapids, MI: Phanes Press, 1997).

Connelly, Joan Breton. *The Parthenon Enigma* (New York: Alfred A. Knopf, 2014).

Conway, D. J. *Animal Magick* (Woodbury, MN: Llewellyn Publications, 1995).

—————. *Magickal Mermaids and Water Creatures: Invoke the Magick of the Waters* (Newburyport, MA: New Page Books, 2005).

—————. *Magickal Mystical Creatures: Invite Their Powers into Your Life* (Woodbury, MN: Llewellyn Publications, 2018).

Cooke, Bill, "The Horse in Chinese History." In Cooke, 2000, pp. 27–62.

—————, dir. *Imperial China: The Art of the Horse in Chinese History*, exh. cat. (Lexington, KY: Kentucky Horse Park; in conjunction with Prospect, KY: Harmony House Publishers, 2000).

Crowley, Aleister, Hymenaeus Beta, and Samuel Liddell MacGregor Mathers, trans. and ed. *The Goetia: The Lesser Key of Solomon the King: Lemegeton—Clavicula Salomonis Regis, Book 1* (Boston: Red Wheel, 1995).

Davidson, Hilda R. E. *Myths and Symbols in Pagan Europe: Early Scandinavian and Celtic Religions* (Manchester, England: Manchester University Press, 1988).

Dawson, Tess. *The Horned Altar: Rediscovering and Rekindling Canaanite Magick* (Woodbury, MN: Llewellyn Publications, 2013).

DiLuzio, Meghan J. *A Place at the Altar: Priestesses in Republican Rome* (Princeton, NJ: Princeton University Press, 2016).

Drews, Robert. *Early Riders: The Beginnings of Mounted Warfare in Asia and Europe* (New York: Routledge Press, 2004).

Duczko, Wladyslaw. *Viking Rus: Studies on the Presence of Scandinavians in Eastern Europe* (Leiden, Netherlands: Brill, 2004).

DuQuette, Lon Milo. *Tarot of Ceremonial Magick: A Pictorial Synthesis of Three Great Pillars of Magick (Astrology, Enochian Magick, Goetia)* (York Beach, ME: Samuel Weiser, Inc., 1995).

Fraschetti, Augusto. *Roman Women*, trans. Linda Lappin (Chicago: University of Chicago Press, 2001).

Freud, Sigmund. *The Interpretation of Dreams*, trans. A. A. Brill (Digireads. com Publishing, 2017).

Froehlich, David J. "Quo vadis eohippus? The Systematics and Taxonomy of the Early Eocene Equids (Perissodactyla)," *Zoological Journal of the Linnean Society* 134 (2) (February 2002), pp. 141–256.

Gaunitz, C., et al. "Ancient Genomes Revisit the Ancestry of Domestic and Przewalski's Horses," *Science Magazine* 360 (6384) (April 6, 2018), pp. 111–114.

Gauvard, Claude, Alain de Libera, Michel Zink, dirs. *Dictionnaire du Moyen Âge* (Paris: Quadrige/Presses Universitaires de France, 2002).

GaWaNi Pony Boy. *Horse, Follow Closely: Native American Horsemanship* (Irvine, CA: Bow Tie Press, 1998).

Godwin, David. *Godwin's Cabalistic Encyclopedia: Complete Guide to Both Practical and Esoteric Applications*, 3rd ed. (Woodbury, MN: Llewellyn Publications, 2003).

Hall, Judy. *The Crystal Bible* (Cincinnati, OH: Walking Stick Press, 2016).

Hausman, Gerald, and Loretta Hausman. *The Mythology of Horses: Horse Legend and Lore throughout the Ages* (New York: Three Rivers Press, 2003).

Hermes, Nizar F. "Utter Alterity or Pure Humanity: Barbarian Turks, Bulghars, and Rus (Vikings) in the Remarkable *Risala* of Ibn Fadlan." In *The [European] Other in Medieval Arabic Literature and Culture: Ninth-Twelfth Century AD* (New York: Palgrave Macmillan, 2012), pp. 80–84.

Howey, Mary Gertrude Oldfield. *The Horse in Magic and Myth* (London: William Rider & Sons, Ltd., 1923; reprint, Mineola, NY: Dover Publications, 2002).

Hughes, Kristoffer. *From the Cauldron Born: Exploring the Magic of Welsh Legend and Lore* (Woodbury, MN: Llewellyn, 2017).

Hyland, Ann. *The Horse in the Middle Ages* (Thrupp, England: Sutton Publishing, 1999).

Illes, Judika. *Encyclopedia of 5,000 Spells: The Ultimate Reference Book for the Magical Arts* (New York: HarperOne, 2009).

——————. *Encyclopedia of Mystics, Saints & Sages: A Guide to Asking for Protection, Wealth, Happiness, and Everything Else!* (New York: HarperOne, 2011).

——————. *Encyclopedia of Witchcraft: The Complete A-Z for the Entire Magical World* (London: HarperCollins, 2005).

Ivantchik, Askold. "The Funeral of Scythian Kings: The Historical Reality and the Description of Herodotus (IV, 71–72)." In L. Bonfante, ed., *The Barbarians of Ancient Europe* (Cambridge, England: Cambridge University Press, 2011), pp. 71–106.

Jaang, L., Z. Sun, J. Shao, and M. Li. "When Peripheries Were Centres: A Preliminary Study of the Shimao-centred Polity in the Loess Highland, China," *Antiquity* 92 (364) (2018), pp. 1008–1022.

Jansen, Thomas, et al. "Mitochondrial DNA and the Origins of the Domestic Horse," *Proceedings of the National Academy of Sciences of the United States of America* 99.16 (2002), pp. 10905–10910.

Jarus, Owen. "Massive Pyramid, Lost City and Ancient Human Sacrifices Unearthed in China," *Live Science* (August 23, 2018). Retrieved from *https://livescience.com* (accessed 1/12/2019).

Jenkins, Ian. *The Parthenon Frieze* (Austin, TX: University of Texas Press, 1994).

——————. *The Parthenon Sculptures* (Cambridge, MA: Harvard University Press, 2007).

Johns, Andreas. *Baba Yaga: The Ambiguous Mother and Witch of the Russian Folktale* (New York: Peter Lang Inc., International Academic Publishers; First Edition edition, 2004).

Johnston, Sarah Iles. *Religions of the Ancient World: A Guide* (Cambridge, MA: The Belknap Press of Harvard University Press, 2004).

Jung, C. G. *The Archetypes and the Collective Unconscious*, trans. R. F. C. Hull, 2nd ed. (Princeton, NJ: Princeton University Press, 1981).

——————. *Dreams*, trans. R. F. C. Hull, rev. ed. (Princeton, NJ: Princeton University Press, 2010).

Kaiser, Anton. *Joan of Arc: A Study in Charismatic Women's Leadership* (Rapid City, SD: Black Hills Books, 2017).

Kehnel, Annette. "Le sacrifice du cheval." In Bernard Andenmatten, Agostino Paravicini Bagliani et Eva Pibiri, ed., *Le cheval dans la culture médiévale* (Florence, Italy: SISMEL Edizioni del Galluzzo, 2015), pp. 5–32.

King, Leonard W. *Babylonian Magic and Sorcery* (York Beach, ME: Weiser, 2000; reprint of 1896).

Lavers, Chris. *The Natural History of Unicorns* (New York: HarperCollins, 2009).

Lawrence, Robert Means. *The Magic of the Horse Shoe with Other Folklore Notes* (Boston: Houghton, Mifflin, and Co., 1898).

Lecouteux, Claude. *Dictionary of Gypsy Mythology: Charms, Rites, and Magical Traditions of the Roma*, trans. Jon E. Graham (Rochester, VT: Inner Traditions, 2018).

——————. *A Lapidary of Sacred Stones: Their Magical and Medicinal Powers Based on the Earliest Sources*, trans. Jon E. Graham (Rochester, VT: Inner Traditions, 2012).

——————. *Phantom Armies of the Night: The Wild Hunt and the Ghostly Processions of the Undead*, trans. Jon E. Graham (Rochester, VT: Inner Traditions, 2011).

——————. *The Tradition of Household Spirits: Ancestral Lore and Practices*, trans. Jon E. Graham (Rochester, VT: Inner Traditions, 2013).

Lenormant, François. *Chaldean Magic: Its Origin and Development* (York Beach, ME: Weiser, 1999; reprint of 1878).

Leo, Lawren. *Dragonflame: Tap into Your Resrervoir of Power Using Talismans, Manifestation, and Visualization* (Pompton Plains, NJ: New Page Books, 2014).

Linduff, Katheryn. "Epona: A Celt among the Romans," *Latoma* 38, 4 (1979), pp. 817–837.

Lomand, Ulla, "The Horse and Its Role in Icelandic Burial Practices, Mythology, and Society." In Anders Andren, Kristina Jennbert, and Catharina Raudvere, ed., *Old Norse Religion in Long-term Perspectives: Origins, Changes, and Interactions* (Lund, Sweden: Nordic Academic, 2006), pp. 130–133.

Long, Carolyn Morrow. *A New Orleans Voudou Priestess: The Legend and Reality of Marie Laveau* (Gainesville, FL: University Press of Florida, 2006).

Lunde, Paul, and Caroline Stone. *Ibn Fadlan and the Land of Darkness: Arab Travellers in the Far North* (London: Penguin Classics, 2011).

MacFadden, Bruce J. *Fossil Horses: Systematics, Paleobiology, and Evolution of the Family Equidae* (Cambridge, England: Cambridge University Press, 1994).

McCarriston, Linda. "La Coursier de Jeanne d'Arc." In *Little River: New and Selected Poems* (Knockeven, Ireland: Salmon Poetry, 1993); available in full online at: *https://poets.org* (accessed 12/15/2018).

Meeks, Dimitri. "L'introduction du cheval en Égypte et son insertion dans les croyances religieuses." In Armelle Gardeisen, ed., *Les équidés dans le monde méditerranéen antique* (Lattes, France: CNRS, 2005), pp. 51–59.

Meltzer, Françoise. *For Fear of the Fire: Joan of Arc and the Limits of Subjectivity* (Chicago: Chicago University Press, 2001).

Mitchell, Stephen A. *Witchcraft and Magic in the Norse Middle Ages* (Philadelphia: University of Pennsylvania Press, 2010).

Naumann, Nelly. "*Sakahagi*: The 'Reverse Flaying' of the Heavenly Piebald Horse," *Asian Folklore Studies* 41 (1982), pp. 7–38.

Neils, Jennifer. *Goddess and Polis: The Panathenaic Festival in Ancient Athens* (Princeton, NJ: Princeton University Press, 1992).

——————. *The Parthenon: From Antiquity to the Present* (Cambridge, England: Cambridge University Press, 2005).

Ni, Xueting Christine. *From Kuan Yin to Chairman Mao: The Essential Guide to Chinese Deities* (Newburyport, MA: Weiser Books, 2018).

O'Donnell, James H. *Ohio's First Peoples* (Athens, OH: Ohio University Press, 2004).

Orlando, Ludovic, et al. "Recalibrating *Equus* Evolution Using the Genome Sequence of an Early Middle Pleistocene Horse," *Nature* 499 (July 4, 2013), pp. 74–78.

O'Daniel Cantrell, Deborah. *The Horsemen of Israel: Horses and Chariotry in Monarchic Israel (Ninth-Eighth Centuries BCE)* (Winona Lake, IN: Eisenbrauns, 2011).

Outram, Alan K., et al. "The Earliest Horse Harnessing and Milking," *Science* 323 (March 2009), pp. 1332–1335.

Owen, D. I. "The First Equestrian: An Ur III Glyptic Scene," *Acta Sumerologica* 13 (1991), pp. 259–273.

Page, R. I. *Chronicles of the Vikings: Records, Memorials, and Myths* (Toronto: University of Toronto Press, 1995).

Pearson, Nicholas. *The Seven Archetypal Stones: Their Spiritual Powers and Teachings* (Rochester, VT: Inner Traditions, 2016).

Pepper, Elizabeth and Barbara Stacy. *The Little Book of Magical Creatures*, rev. ed. (Providence, RI: The Witches' Almanac, 2009).

Price, Steve. *America's Wild Horses: The History of the Western Mustang* (New York: Skyhorse Publishing, 2017).

Ramsay, Nigel. *St. Dunstan: His Life, Times, and Cult* (Rochester, NY: Boydell Press, 1992).

Raulwing, Peter, ed. and trans. *The Kikkuli Text. Hittite Training Instructions for Chariot Horses in the Second Half of the 2nd Millennium B.C. and Their Interdisciplinary Context* (text published directly online, 2009). Retrieved from *http://www.lrgaf.org* (accessed 9/26/2019).

Recht, Laerke, "Asses Were Buried with Him: Equids as Markers of Sacred Space in the Third and Second Millennia BC in the Eastern Mediterranean." In Louis Daniel Nebelsick, et al., ed., *Sacred Space: Contributions to the Archaeology of Belief* (Archaeologica Hereditas, 13) (Warsaw, Poland: Institute of Archaeology, Cardinal Stefan Wyszyński University, 2018), pp. 65–94.

Rich, Janet Bubar. *Riding on Horses' Wings: Reimagining Today's Horse for Tomorrow's World* (New York: Peter Lang Publishing, Inc., 2016).

Rowsell, Thomas. "Riding to the Afterlife: The Role of Horses in Early Medieval North-Western Europe," MA Thesis, University College of London, 2012.

Russell, Jeffrey Burton. *Witchcraft in the Middle Ages* (Ithaca, NY: Cornell University Press, 1972).

Seward, Desmond. *The Hundred Years War: The English in France 1337–1453* (New York and London: Penguin Books, 1999).

Shai, Itzhaq, et al. "The Importance of the Donkey as a Pack Animal in the Early Bronze Age Southern Levant: A View from *Tell eṣ-Ṣfil Gath*," *Zeitschrift des Deutschen Palästina-Vereins* 132 (2016), pp. 1–25.

Shenk, Peter. *To Valhalla by Horseback? Horse Burial in Scandinavia during the Viking Age* (Oslo, Norway: The Center for Viking and Medieval Studies, University of Oslo, 2002).

Singer, Ben. "A Brief History of the Horse in America: Horse Phylogeny and Evolution," *Canadian Geographic* (May 2005). Retrieved from *https://web.archive.org* (accessed 1/13/2019).

Snow, Dean. "Sexual Dimorphism in European Upper Paleolithic Cave Art," *American Antiquity* 78 (4), (2013), pp. 746–761.

Todeschi, Kevin J. *Edgar Cayce on Soul Symbolism: Creating Life Seals, Aura Charts, and Understanding the Revelation* (Virginia Beach, VA: Yazdan Publishing, 2015).

Van Auken, John. *Edgar Cayce on the Revelation: A Study Guide for Spiritualizing Body and Mind* (New York: Sterling, 2005).

Vögelin, Carl F., and E. W. Vögelin. "Shawnee Name Groups," *American Anthropologist* 37 issue 4 (October–December 1935), pp. 617–635.

Waddell, John. "Equine Cults and Celtic Goddesses," *Emania Bulletin of the Navan Research Group* 24 (2018), pp. 5–18.

Ward, Martha. *Voodoo Queen: The Spirited Lives of Marie Laveau* (Oxford, Mississippi: University of Mississippi Press, 2004).

Warner, Marina. *Joan of Arc: The Image of Female Heroism* (Oxford, England: Oxford University Press, 1981).

Williams, Wendy. *The Horse: The Epic History of Our Noble Companion* (New York: Scientific American / Farrar, Straus, and Giroux, 2015).

Winkle, Jeffrey T. "Epona Salvatrix? Isis and the Horse Goddess in Apuleius' *Metamorphoses*," *Ancient Narrative* 12 (2015).

Zivie-Coche, Christiane, "Foreign Deities in Egypt." In Jacco Dieleman and Willeke Wendrich, eds., *UCLA Encyclopedia of Egyptology* (Los Angeles, 2011). Retrieved from *https://escholarship.org* (accessed 3/15/2018).

# INDEX

# ABOUT THE AUTHORS

**Lawren Leo** is a psychic and author of several books, including the magickal primer, *Dragonflame: Tap into Your Reservoir of Power Using Talismans, Manifestation, and Visualization* (New Page Books, 2014) and a collection of short stories, *Love's Shadow: Nine Crooked Paths* (2015). He is also owner of New Moon Books, Crystals, and Candles, Inc., a metaphysical boutique in Pompano Beach, Florida. He contributes to and coedits the e-zine he founded, *The Familiar*. He studied classical piano at Pepperdine University and went on to work in the world of advertising, but subsequently left to travel Europe, North Africa, and the Middle East to prepare himself for his true calling—a life of spiritual counseling, the study of esoteric philosophy, and the practice of the magickal arts in the tradition of the Golden Dawn.

**Domenic Leo, PhD,** holds degrees in French and Spanish Literature, Linguistics, and Ancient Greek, Early Christian, Islamic, and Medieval Art History from Georgetown University, Christie's Education, and New York University's Institute of Fine Arts. He taught art history at Duquesne University, Youngstown State University, and The Art Institute of Pittsburgh Online Division, and has lectured throughout the United States, Great Britain, and Europe. His publications are numerous and award-winning. He is also the buyer for New Moon Books, Crystals, and Candles, Inc., in Pompano Beach, Florida, where he edits the e-zine, *The Familiar*. He has lived abroad researching and writing in London, Paris, Fiesole, and Berlin and has traveled around the world.

Both Leo brothers have been equestrians and horse lovers from their early teens.

# TO OUR READERS

Weiser Books, an imprint of Red Wheel/Weiser, publishes books across the entire spectrum of occult, esoteric, speculative, and New Age subjects. Our mission is to publish quality books that will make a difference in people's lives without advocating any one particular path or field of study. We value the integrity, originality, and depth of knowledge of our authors.

Our readers are our most important resource, and we appreciate your input, suggestions, and ideas about what you would like to see published.

Visit our website at *www.redwheelweiser.com* to learn about our upcoming books and free downloads, and be sure to go to *www.redwheelweiser.com/newsletter* to sign up for newsletters and exclusive offers.

You can also contact us at *info@rwwbooks.com* or at

Red Wheel/Weiser, LLC
65 Parker Street, Suite 7
Newburyport, MA 01950